Easy-to-make
Outdoor
Furniture

By the Editors of Sunset Books and Sunset Magazine

Lane Publishing Co. · Menlo Park, California

Furniture for your patio or garden ... portable, storable, durable

You provide the time, tools, and materials—this book will guide you step by step through the making of outdoor furniture.

Flip through the pages to find a project that looks right for you. You'll find an assortment of materials, styles, and degrees of simplicity. The furniture pieces are of plain materials, honestly used, and each has been selected because of its practical nature. All are either portable and storable during off-season months or durable enough to brave foul weather.

To avoid repetition in the directions for each project, we've included in the back of the book a section entitled "Materials and Techniques" that offers general information and methods used in several projects.

For their help, we thank Art Center School of Design, Art Bonner, Domus of Bellevue, Arnie Goedecke, Duane Haggerty, Bill Kapranos, Ron Rezek, and Bo Tegelvik.

Edited by Donald W. Vandervort

Staff Assistants: Don Rutherford, Jim Barrett

Design: Al Ackers

Illustrations: Mark Pechenik, AIA

Photography: All photographs in this book are by Ells Marugg, with the following exceptions: pages 43–45, Norman A. Plate; page 54, Roger Schreiber; page 29, Don Vandervort; page 21, Darrow M. Watt.

Cover: Casual chair—directions on page 30; rolling patio pallets—directions on page 12. Photographed by Ells Marugg.

Editor, Sunset Books: David E. Clark

Fourth printing October 1982

Contents

Nesting Boxes

Modular staging for people and plants

Nesting Boxes

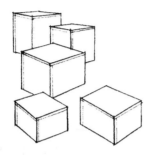

Grouped, these easy-to-make modular boxes serve as a picnic table and benches of varying sizes, creating the pleasing effect of enclosed space and random levels. Placed side by side, they make a formal setting for potted plants. Children are attracted to them like cats to a paper bag—for kids, the boxes become oversize building blocks or props for a backyard theater.

Best of all, these boxes nest compactly and are easily wheeled away on their own cart for storage when not in use.

Though the boxes shown were made of $\frac{5}{8}''$ exterior rough-sawn plywood siding, a less expensive exterior plywood can be used where appearance is less important than economy.

Design: Rick Morrall

Tools you'll need:
pencil · measuring tape · square · crosscut saw or power circular saw · hammer · nailset (or large nail) · screwdriver · wire brush or coarse sandpaper and finishing tools. *Helpful tools* include a table saw or radial-arm saw and a power sander with coarse sandpaper.

Unstacked, nesting boxes accommodate groups or create intimate settings.

One on top of the other, nesting boxes stack and roll away for easy, minimum-space storage.

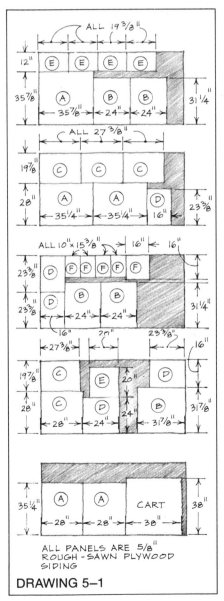

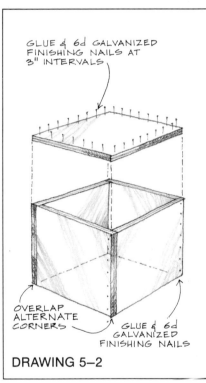

Materials list

5 sheets $\frac{5}{8}''$ rough-sawn plywood siding, 4' by 8'
2 pounds of 6d (2'') galvanized finishing nails
4 pivoting outdoor casters, $2\frac{1}{2}''$, with $\frac{5}{8}''$ screws
Waterproof resorcinol glue
Exterior wood stain or clear polyurethane finish

Here's How

Begin by cutting the various pieces of plywood to size, as specified in drawing 5-1, using a square to mark and check all cuts. (If you prefer, you may be able to have the lumberyard attendant make the major cuts for a minimal fee.) Save the plywood scraps for making small boxes or other outdoor projects.

Assemble the sides and top of each of the six boxes (labeled A through F), overlapping the corners as shown in drawing 5-2. Spread glue along the joining surfaces and nail with 6d galvanized finishing nails, spacing the nails about 3'' apart. Set the nails below the surface. Screw casters to the four corners of the piece marked "cart." To make an easier job of rolling the cart on rough terrain, consider nailing 1 by 2s around three of its edges (see photo above).

To reduce splinters from the rough-sawn siding, sweep with a wire brush or sand with coarse sandpaper. Apply wood stain or clear polyurethane finish. Cushions can be added for more comfortable seating (for information on making cushions, see page 76).

Bench from 2 by 6 Decking (see facing page)

Sturdy Plank Bench (see page 8)

Take-apart Redwood Bench (see page 9)

Benches

These are sturdy and easy to build

Bench from 2 by 6 Decking

(Photo on facing page)

Because it is made entirely of 2 by 6 decking, this bench is a perfect complement for many outdoor decks. And construction is simple: you just make a few straight cuts with a saw and nail the pieces together.
Design: Don Vandervort

Tools you'll need:

pencil · measuring tape · square · crosscut saw or power circular saw · hammer · sandpaper and finishing tools. *Helpful tools* include a table saw or radial-arm saw and a drill with a $\frac{1}{8}''$ bit.

Materials list

38' of 2 by 6 Select redwood decking: 3 @ 10', 1 @ 8'
1 pound of 16d ($3\frac{1}{2}''$) galvanized common (or finishing) nails
Clear polyurethane exterior finish

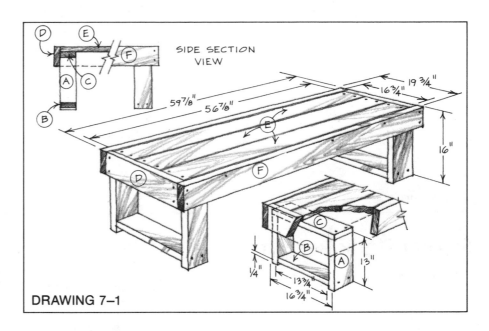

DRAWING 7–1

Here's How

Begin by cutting the various pieces to length according to the following cutting list (refer to drawing 7-1). Be sure to use a square for marking and checking your cuts. Cut all (A), (C), and (D) pieces from one 10-footer; cut both (B) lengths and one (E) piece from an 8-footer; cut the other two (E) pieces from a 10-footer; and cut both (F) lengths from a 10-footer.

(A) Four 2 by 6s, 13''
(B) Two 2 by 6s, $13\frac{3}{4}''$
(C) and (D) Four 2 by 6s, $16\frac{3}{4}''$
(E) Three 2 by 6s, $56\frac{7}{8}''$
(F) Two 2 by 6s, $59\frac{7}{8}''$

Nail together the (A), (B), and (C) pieces to make up the two leg-support assemblies, as shown in drawing 7-1. Use two 16d galvanized nails per joint.

Next, connect the two leg assemblies by nailing the (E) pieces to them through (C), flush with (C) at both ends and edges, and spaced evenly. To avoid splitting, it helps to predrill nail holes through (E), and also through (F), with a $\frac{1}{8}''$ bit. Align the nails carefully; use two at each end of each (E) piece.

Then nail (D) and (F) around the perimeter: Nail (D) to (A) with two nails at each end; nail (F) to (D) with two nails at each end. Add three or four nails through (F) into (E), spaced evenly.

Sand lightly, rounding edges and corners. Apply two coats of clear polyurethane exterior finish.

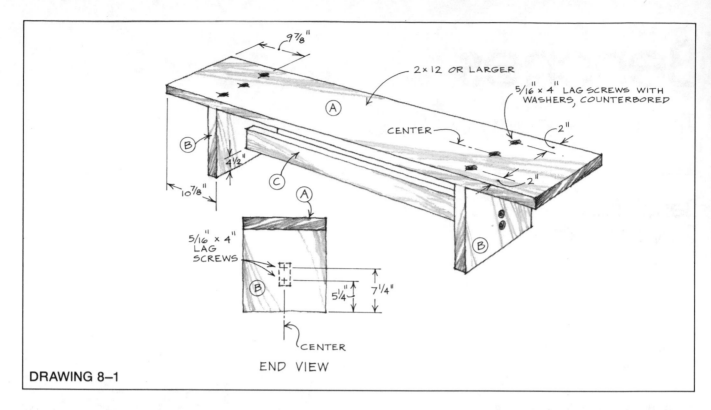

9⅞"

2×12 OR LARGER

5/16" × 4" LAG SCREWS WITH WASHERS, COUNTERBORED

Ⓐ

CENTER

2"

Ⓑ

4½"

Ⓒ

10⅞"

2"

Ⓐ

Ⓑ

5/16" × 4" LAG SCREWS

Ⓑ

Ⓑ

5¼"

7¼"

CENTER

END VIEW

DRAWING 8–1

Sturdy Plank Bench

(Photo on page 6)

This bench is probably the easiest to make of all the projects in this book. Once you purchase the materials, all you do is make three simple saw cuts, fasten the boards together, and finish the wood. The bench's width is determined by the width of planks you buy; sizes from 2 by 12 to 2 by 16 are the best choices. The bench in the photo is made from a 2 by 12.

Tools you'll need:

pencil • measuring tape • square • crosscut saw or power circular saw • drill with ¼" and 1" bits • ½" wrench • wire brush • coarse sandpaper and finishing tools. *Helpful tools* include a radial-arm saw, ½" socket wrench, and power sander.

Materials list

8' of 2 by 12, 14, or 16 rough cedar or redwood
4' of 2 by 4 rough cedar or redwood
10 zinc-plated lag screws, $\frac{5}{16}$" by 4", with washers
Clear polyurethane exterior finish

Here's How

Begin by cutting the 2 by 12 (or larger) plank into three pieces: one 69¾" long (A) and two 13" long (B). Use a square to mark and check all saw cuts.

Next, mark placement of six screw holes on the large plank (A), as detailed in drawing 8-1. At these locations, counterbore 1"-diameter holes ⅜" deep for recessing the lag screw heads and washers. Then drill ¼" pilot holes all the way through

(A), centered in each counterbored hole. Hold the legs (B) in place at proper locations and drill down into their top ends through the holes in (A) (a helper will come in handy for this job).

Next, thread a lag screw through a washer and, using a wrench, drive it down into (B) through one lag screw hole in (A). Repeat for the other five lag-screw holes.

Measure the exact distance between the two legs (it will be about 48") and cut the 2 by 4 (C) to that exact length. On legs (B), mark lag screw locations as detailed in the end view. As you did through (A), counterbore and drill lag screw pilot holes through (B) into (C). Drive in lag screws.

Give all wood a good wire brushing in the direction of the wood grain to remove splinters, then sand with coarse sandpaper. Apply two coats of clear polyurethane exterior finish.

Take-apart Redwood Bench

(Photo on page 6)

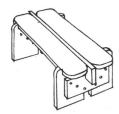

Here's a good-looking, sturdy bench that comes apart for easy storage. It's simple to make from standard lumber—the redwood 2 by 8s and 2 by 10s are simply bolted together; the bench can be taken apart or assembled with interlocking joints (see drawing 9-1).
Design: Don Vandervort

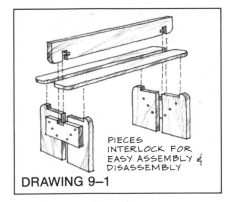

PIECES INTERLOCK FOR EASY ASSEMBLY & DISASSEMBLY

DRAWING 9–1

Tools you'll need:

pencil · measuring tape · square · compass · keyhole or coping saw · crosscut saw or power circular saw · chisel · rasp · drill with a $\frac{5}{16}''$ bit · hammer · $\frac{1}{2}''$ wrench · sandpaper and finishing tools. *Helpful tools* include a table saw or radial-arm saw, saber saw, drill press, and power sander.

Materials list

14' of 2 by 8 redwood: 2 @ 7'
6' of 2 by 10 redwood
12 zinc-plated carriage bolts, $\frac{5}{16}''$ by $3\frac{1}{2}''$, with washers and nuts
Polyurethane penetrating oil-sealer finish

Here's How

Begin by cutting all the parts to size, as specified in the following cutting list (also refer to drawing 9-2). Be sure to mark and check all cuts with a square.

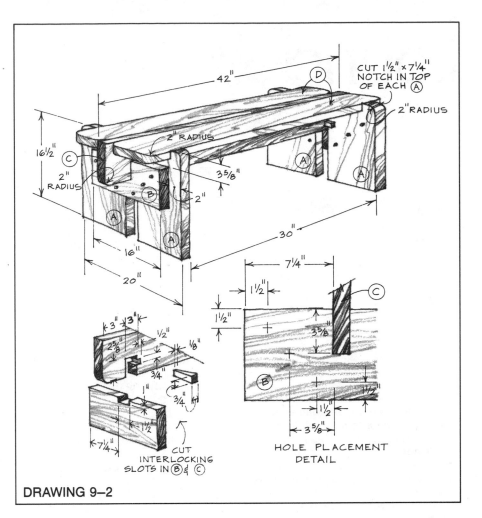

DRAWING 9–2

Cut all (A) from the 2 by 10; cut both (B) and one (C) from one 2 by 8; and cut both (D) from the other 2 by 8.

(A) Four 2 by 10s, $16\frac{1}{2}''$
(B) Two 2 by 8s, 16"
(C) and (D) Three 2 by 8s, 42"

Mark and cut the $1\frac{1}{2}''$ by $7\frac{1}{4}''$ notches in the tops of (A) and the slots in (B) and (C) as shown in the drawings. Use a chisel and a rasp to remove excess wood from these notches and slots. For more about making interlocking joints and cutting slots, see pages 69 and 74. Use a compass to mark the rounded corners of (A), (C), and (D), then cut them, using a keyhole saw, coping saw, or saber saw.

Next, mark placement of bolt holes on (B), according to the detail above. Drill these $\frac{5}{16}''$ holes through (B). Then align the two (A) pieces that make up each end, flush at top and bottom, square with each other,

and separated $1\frac{1}{2}''$ (use a scrap $1\frac{1}{2}''$-thick block as a spacer). Use the respective (B) pieces for marking hole placement with the drill. Remove (B) and drill all the way through (A).

Pound carriage bolts through (B) into (A). Add washers and tighten on nuts. Slide (C) into place, interlocking with both assembled ends, and lay both (D) pieces in the notches on the tops of (A) and snug against (C) to check for fit. If any cuts must be made a little wider or deeper, do that now.

Lift off (D) and (C). Sand all pieces, wipe clean, and apply two coats of polyurethane penetrating oil-sealer finish. Let dry, then reassemble. From scrap wood, cut or carve two tapered wedges as detailed. Tap these into the wedge slots to draw the unit tightly together.

Lounges

Three that follow the sun

Adjustable Sun Lounge

(Photo on facing page)

One great pleasure of summer is basking in the sun on a full-length chaise. This updated classic is comfortable, sturdy, and mobile—it rolls around easily to follow the sun's ever-moving arc. The backrest is adjustable, and because of the lounge's slender shape, it stores in a minimum of space.

Design: Gordon Hammond

Tools you'll need:

pencil · measuring tape · square · crosscut saw or power circular saw · hacksaw · drill with a $\frac{7}{64}$″ bit · hammer · nailset (or large nail) · screwdriver · sandpaper and finishing tools. *Helpful tools* include a table saw or radial-arm saw and a power sander.

Materials list

All hardware and fastenings should be rust-resistant.

14′ of 1 by 4 fir: 2 @ 7′
4′ of 1 by 2 fir
12′ of $\frac{3}{4}$″ by $\frac{3}{4}$″ molding
6′ of $\frac{1}{4}$″ by $\frac{3}{4}$″ screen molding
1 sheet of $\frac{1}{2}$″ exterior plywood, 4′ by 8′
4′ of continuous hinge, with $\frac{1}{2}$″ screws
6 pivoting outdoor casters, 2″
16 roundhead screws, 1$\frac{1}{4}$″ by #12
8 roundhead screws, $\frac{1}{2}$″ by #12
2 dozen $\frac{1}{2}$″ brads

1 pound each of 3d (1$\frac{1}{4}$″) and 6d (2″) finishing nails
Waterproof resorcinol glue
Wood filler (fir)
Enamel paint
Standard 2′ by 6′ chaise pad (purchase at an outdoor furniture store)

Here's How

Before you cut out the pieces, be sure you can locate a store that sells chaise pads that are a full 2′ by 6′. Otherwise, you'll need to revise the measurements to fit the size pad available to you.

Begin by cutting the various pieces to size (refer to drawings 10-1 and 11-2). For the plywood pieces (A through F), follow the cutting diagram (drawing 11-1). Use a square to mark and check all cuts. If you don't have a power saw, you may be able to have the lumberyard

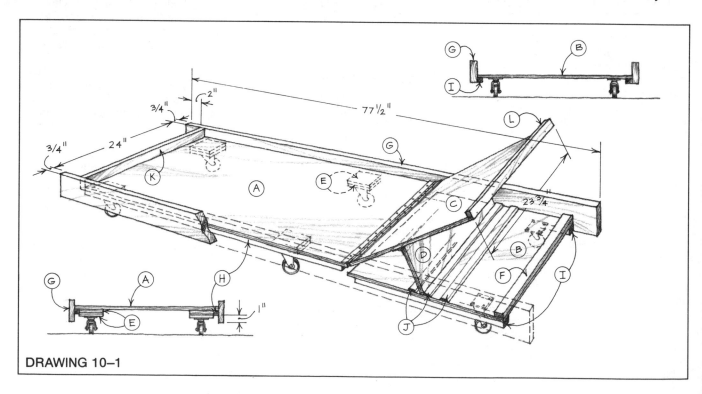

DRAWING 10–1

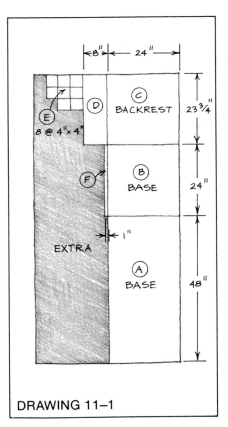

DRAWING 11–1

Adjustable Sun Lounge (see facing page)

attendant make the major cuts for a minimal charge. Here are the other pieces you'll need:

(G) Two 1 by 4s, $77\frac{1}{2}''$
(H) Two $\frac{3}{4}''$ by $\frac{3}{4}''$ pieces, 47''
(I) Two $\frac{3}{4}''$ by $\frac{3}{4}''$ pieces, 23''
(J) Three $\frac{1}{4}''$ by $\frac{3}{4}''$ pieces, 24''
(K) One 1 by 2, 24''
(L) One 1 by 2, $23\frac{3}{4}''$

Glue and nail the rails (H and I) to the sides (G), using 3d nails. As you can see in drawing 10-1, the short rails (I) fit flush with the bottom of the sides (G). The long rails (H) are raised 1'' from the lower edges of the sides.

Glue and nail the $23\frac{3}{4}''$ end strip (L) to the backrest (C), using 6d nails. Then glue and nail the 24'' end strip (K) to the base (A), using 6d nails. With glue and 3d nails, fasten the two bases (A and B) to the rails.

With a hacksaw, cut two $23\frac{3}{4}''$ lengths of continuous hinge. Use one to fasten the backrest prop (D) to the backrest (C), 8'' from the end that will hinge to the base (A). (See drawing 11-2.) Attach the backrest (C) to the base (A) with the other length of the hinge.

Glue (E) pieces together in pairs to form four caster pads. Glue and nail pads to the bottom of base (A) inside the rails, two at the foot, and two 10'' from the hinge (see drawing

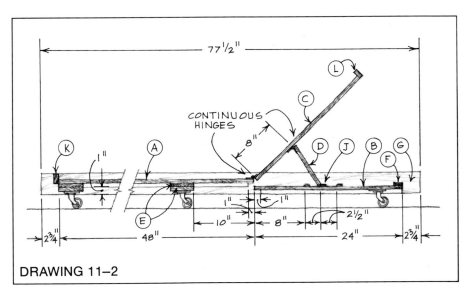

DRAWING 11–2

10-1). After drilling $\frac{7}{64}''$ pilot holes, screw casters to pads, using $1\frac{1}{4}''$ screws. Then, drilling pilot holes and using $\frac{1}{2}''$ screws, attach the other two casters to the head end of base (B), positioned in the corners 2'' in from the edges.

Glue and attach with $\frac{1}{2}''$ brads a $\frac{1}{4}'' \times \frac{3}{4}''$ strip (J) across (B), 8'' from the inward end of (B), as shown in drawing 10-1. Attach the other two strips (J) to give backrest angles that are comfortable for you—spacing them about $2\frac{1}{2}''$ apart. Also

glue and nail (F) in place, flat and flush with the edge of (B), where shown in the drawing.

Set the nails below the surface and fill. Sand the wood surfaces until smooth. Paint the chaise with two or three coats of enamel, lightly sanding between coats. Let the paint dry, put the cushion in place, and enjoy!

Patio pallets provide individual seating; lined up, they become a lounge.

Rolling Patio Pallets

These patio pallets lead a double life. As individual seats, they roll around the patio to follow the crowd. Joined in a string of three, they become a comfortable lounge for sunbathing by the pool. Because they're relatively inexpensive and quite easy to make, you may want several sets.

Design: Gordon Hammond

Tools you'll need:

pencil · measuring tape · square · wood file or rasp · crosscut saw or power circular saw · hammer · nailset (or large nail) · screwdriver · sandpaper and finishing tools · sewing equipment and a sewing machine · serrated bread knife. *Helpful tools* include C-clamps, table saw or radial-arm saw, and electric carving knife.

Materials list (for three pallets)

28' of 1 by 6 fir or pine: 1 @ 12', 2 @ 8'
$\frac{1}{2}$ sheet of $\frac{3}{4}$'' exterior plywood, 4' by 4'
12 pivoting outdoor casters, 2'', with screws
1 pound each of 6d (2'') and 3d ($1\frac{1}{4}$'') galvanized finishing nails
Waterproof resorcinol glue
Wood filler (fir or pine)
Clear polyurethane exterior finish or brightly colored semigloss enamel
5 yards of 30''-wide fabric or equivalent*
Matching thread*
$70\frac{1}{2}$'' by $23\frac{1}{2}$'' of 4''-thick foam*
3 nylon zippers, 22''*
   *You can either make the cushions yourself or have them made at an upholstery shop. If you make the covers, choose a

fabric lightweight enough for your machine to handle.

Here's How

First cut the wooden pieces; be sure to mark and check all cuts with a square. The following list gives the sizes; refer to drawing 13-1. Cut (C) from the 12-footer and (D) from the two 8-footers.

(A) Three $\frac{3}{4}$'' plywood bases, $23\frac{7}{8}$'' square
(B) Twenty-four $\frac{3}{4}$'' plywood caster pads, $4\frac{1}{2}$'' square
(C) Six 1 by 6s, $23\frac{7}{8}$''
(D) Six 1 by 6s, $25\frac{3}{8}$''

Glue and nail together the caster pads (B) in pairs, one pair for each corner of each pallet. Use 3d galvanized finishing nails.

Next, glue and clamp pads to the corners of each plywood base (A), flush with both outer edges. If you don't have clamps, fasten with 6d nails. Let the glue dry thoroughly.

Use a wood file or rasp to smooth the rough plywood edges. Attach the sides (C and D) with glue and 6d nails (see drawing 13-1). Set the nails below the surface and fill.

If your pallets will be left out in the weather, drill four or five ½'' holes in the bases (A) for drainage.

Center the casters on the corner pads and screw them in place. Finish all wood with two coats of clear polyurethane exterior finish or brightly colored enamel.

The cushions are square box cushions. To make them, follow the instructions given under ''Making box cushions,'' page 78.

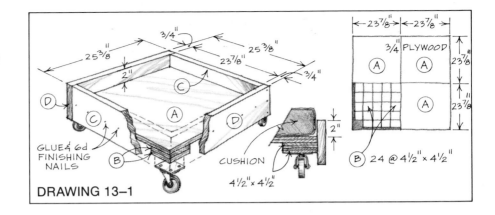

DRAWING 13–1

Wooden Sunning Platform

At home on a deck or at poolside, this sturdy, portable sunning platform is surprisingly comfortable. In addition, it's easy to make. All you do is cut to length a bunch of 1 by 4s, contour a couple of 2 by 8s, and nail the pieces together.
Design: Rick Morrall

Tools you'll need:

pencil • measuring tape • straight-edge • square • crosscut saw • ripsaw or power circular saw • hammer • nailset (or large nail) • sandpaper and finishing tools. If you install casters, you'll also need a drill with a bit sized for caster stem. *Helpful tools* include a table saw or radial-arm saw and a power sander.

Materials list

12' of 2 by 8 fir or pine: 2 @ 6'
46' of 1 by 4 pine: 4 @ 10', 1 @ 6'
1 pound of 8d (2½'') galvanized finishing nails
4 small stem-type outdoor casters (optional)
Wood filler (fir or pine)
Clear exterior polyurethane finish

Here's How

Begin by cutting all 1 by 4s to length—you'll need eighteen at 30''. Be sure to use a square for marking and checking all cuts.

Next, mark and cut the 2 by 8 runners to the shape shown in drawing 13-2. For this cutting, use a ripsaw or power circular saw. Then sand all the wood pieces, rounding off the sharp edges and corners. Finish the pieces with one coat of clear exterior polyurethane finish.

Nail the 1 by 4s to the two 2 by 8 runners with 8d finishing nails, keeping the 1 by 4s flush with the runners at both ends and spaced ½'' apart. Before fastening the last seven 1 by 4s, double-check the spacing and spread any difference over the entire group to assure even spacing.

Set the nails below the surface and fill. When the wood filler dries, sand it smooth and apply a second coat of polyurethane finish to all surfaces.

Small stem-type casters, inserted in holes drilled in the bottom of the runners at all four corners, make the lounge easy to move around.

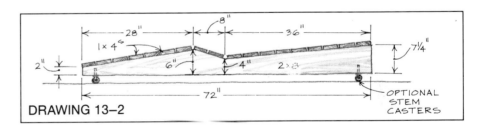

DRAWING 13–2

Sunning platform is contoured for comfort.

Stacking Tripod Modules
(see facing page)

Small Table/Seat
(see page 16)

Redwood Garden Table
(see page 17)

Small Tables

Meeting a variety of needs

Stacking Tripod Modules

(Photo on facing page)

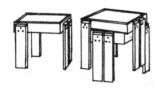

Piggyback, they make a short, tidy stack that requires very little space, but unstack them and these tripod modules serve all sorts of assignments on a deck, patio, or lawn—or indoors.

For storage, you can stack them four high. Unstacked and used individually, they serve as stools or small tables (the "tripod" effect gives them plenty of stability, even on bumpy terrain).
Design: Don Vandervort

Tools you'll need:

pencil • measuring tape • combination square • table saw or radial-arm saw (or substitute a crosscut saw or power circular saw plus a router with a straight bit) • drill with a $\frac{1}{4}''$ bit • $\frac{7}{16}''$ wrench • hammer • nailset (or large nail) • C-clamps • sandpaper and finishing tools. *Helpful tools* include miter clamps, $\frac{7}{16}''$ socket wrench, dado blade, and power sander.

Materials list (for one module)

All hardware and fastenings should be rust-resistant.
11' of 1 by 4 Clear fir
$15\frac{1}{4}''$ by $15\frac{1}{4}''$ of $\frac{1}{2}''$ resawn fir plywood siding
12 carriage bolts, $\frac{1}{4}''$ by 2'', with nuts
24 washers, $\frac{1}{4}''$
2 dozen 4d ($1\frac{1}{2}''$) finishing nails
Waterproof resorcinol glue
Wood filler (fir)
Polyurethane penetrating oil-sealer finish

Here's How

Begin by cutting the 1 by 4s to size. You'll need four at 16'' (A) and four at $15\frac{3}{4}''$ (B) (refer to drawing 15-1). Be sure to use a square for marking and checking all cuts.

Cut the $\frac{3}{8}''$ by $\frac{1}{2}''$ rabbets along one edge of all (A) pieces (either use a dado blade or make three or four passes with a regular power saw blade or a router). Then miter the ends of all (A) pieces at a 45° angle (refer to drawing 15-1 for direction of miters). Also miter one end of each leg (as shown in the drawing).

(Continued on next page)

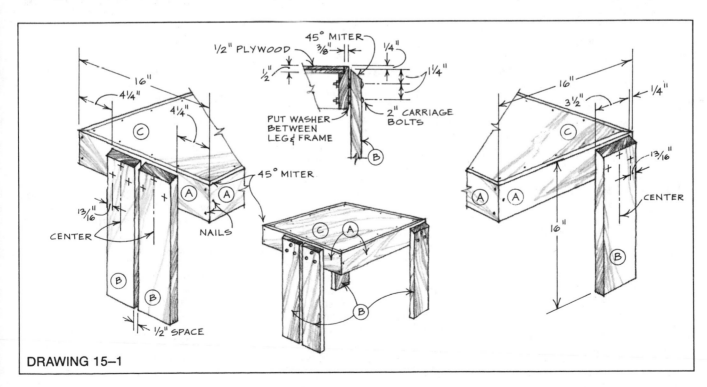

DRAWING 15—1

... *Continued from page 15*

Now join the four (A) pieces in a square. Spread glue on the joining ends of the (A) pieces and secure them together, using miter clamps or C-clamps, as shown on page 73. Add two or three 4d nails at each corner for strength.

Next, measure for and cut the plywood top (C), which should be about 15¼″ square. Spread a small bead of glue around the inner perimeter of the rabbet groove, set the top (C) in place, and nail it with 4d finishing nails. Set all nails and let the glue dry.

See drawing 15-1 for proper placement of the legs (B). Clamp each leg (B) in place. Protect the leg from being damaged by the clamp's jaws by slipping scraps of wood between the jaws and the leg.

Drill ¼″ holes through the legs (B) and the frame (A) at locations specified in drawing 15-1. After drilling each hole, push a carriage bolt through, adding a washer between each leg (B) and the frame (A) and another washer on the bolt's end (inside A); then tighten on a nut.

Fill all nail holes and lightly sand all surfaces in the direction of wood grain. Apply two coats of polyurethane penetrating oil-sealer.

Small Table/Seat

(Photo on page 14)

This versatile table looks at home outdoors no matter where you put it—at poolside, on a deck, in the yard, or on a patio. Sturdy enough to double as a stool or plant stand, it is easy to build and relatively inexpensive; you can build one in a day for under $20.
Design: Jim Barrett

Tools you'll need:

pencil · measuring tape · combination square · crosscut saw or power circular saw · hammer · nailset (or large nail) · sandpaper and finishing tools. *Helpful tools* include a miter box and backsaw, miter clamps, table saw or radial-arm saw, router with a ⅜″-radius bit, and power sander.

Materials list (for one table)

All hardware and fastenings should be rust-resistant.
22′ of 1 by 3 Clear redwood:
  1 @ 10′, 1 @ 8′, 1 @ 4′
6′ of 2 by 2 Clear redwood
3 dozen 2d (1″) finishing nails
5 dozen 3d (1¼″) finishing nails
2 dozen 4d (1½″) finishing nails
Wood filler (redwood)
Waterproof resorcinol glue
Polyurethane penetrating oil-sealer finish

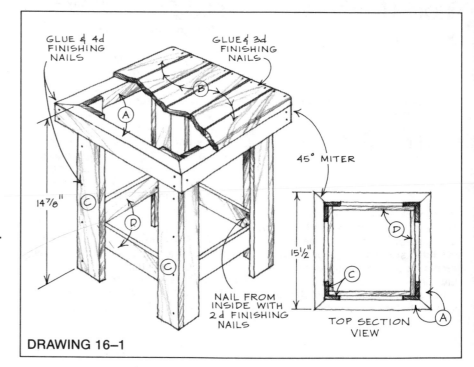

GLUE & 4d FINISHING NAILS

GLUE & 3d FINISHING NAILS

45° MITER

14⅞″

15½″

NAIL FROM INSIDE WITH 2d FINISHING NAILS

TOP SECTION VIEW

DRAWING 16–1

Here's How

Begin by cutting the pieces to length, according to the following cutting list. Use a square for marking and checking all cuts. Cut (B) from the 8-foot 1 by 3, (C) from the 10-footer, and (D) from the 4-footer.

(A) Four 2 by 2s, 15½″
(B) Six 1 by 3s, 15½″
(C) Eight 1 by 3s, 14⅞″
(D) Four 1 by 3s, about 10¼″ (measure and cut later)

Miter the ends of the 2 by 2s (A) at a 45° angle (see drawing 16-1 for direction of miters). Join these in a square, fastening the corners with glue and 4d finishing nails. A miter clamp is handy for aligning and holding the pieces as you nail (see page 73).

Next, glue and nail the top pieces (B) to the square frame with 3d finishing nails, as shown in drawing 16-1. Nail the end pieces first, then space intermediate pieces evenly.

Once you've assembled the top, round off the top edges of the table top with sandpaper or, if you have a router, with a ⅜″-radius bit.

Attach the legs (C) to the top, using glue and 3d finishing nails, nailing through (C) into (A) (refer to drawing 16-1 for positioning). Be sure to keep them perpendicular to the top.

Now cut the leg braces (D), after measuring for exact fit. They should fit snugly against the insides of the legs (C). Glue and nail the braces to the legs, using 2d finishing nails. Set all nails below the surface and fill.

Sand the entire table, rounding off sharp edges. Apply three coats of polyurethane penetrating oil-sealer finish.

Redwood Garden Table

(Photo on page 14)

This small redwood table serves as an outdoor coffee table. Gather around it for casual meals, play games on it, display flowers or plants on it—use it as you see fit. It's a table for all occasions.

When not in use, it quickly disassembles for easy, minimum-space storage. The removable top, made from 1 by 3s, lifts off; the two halves of the base slide apart.

Design: Don Vandervort

Tools you'll need:

pencil · measuring tape · square · crosscut saw or power circular saw · chisel · drill with $\frac{1}{4}''$ and $\frac{7}{8}''$ bits · hammer · two $\frac{7}{16}''$ socket wrenches · sandpaper and finishing tools. *Helpful tools* include a saber saw, table saw or radial-arm saw, dado blade, drill press, C-clamps, and power sander.

Materials list

All hardware and fastenings should be rust-resistant.
16' of 2 by 6 Clear redwood:
  1 @ 10', 1 @ 6'
42' of 1 by 3 Clear redwood:
  1 @ 10', 4 @ 8'
$\frac{1}{4}$ pound of 3d ($1\frac{1}{4}''$) finishing nails
16 machine bolts, $\frac{1}{4}''$ by 4'', with nuts
32 washers, $\frac{1}{4}''$
Waterproof resorcinol glue
Clear polyurethane exterior finish

Here's How

Begin by cutting all the wooden parts to length, according to the following list. Be sure to mark and check all cuts with a square. Cut (A) from the 6'-long 2 by 6; (B) from the 10'-long 2 by 6; all but two of (C) from the 8'-long 1 by 3s; and two (C) plus both (D) from the 10'-long 1 by 3.

(A) Four 2 by 6s, $16\frac{3}{4}''$
(B) Four 2 by 6s, 25''
(C) Fourteen 1 by 3s, 30''
(D) Two 1 by 3s, 25''

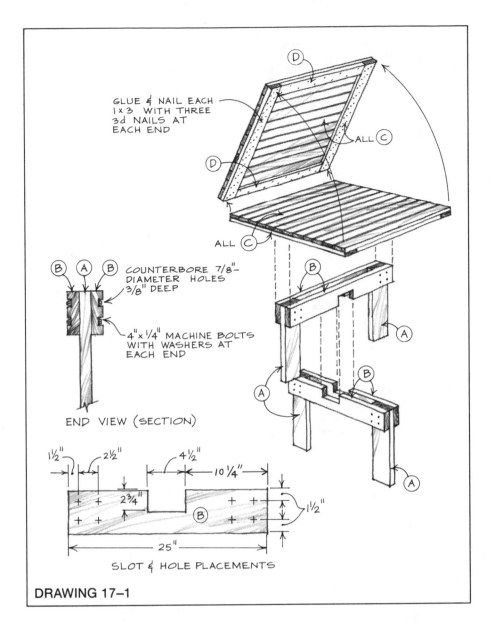

GLUE & NAIL EACH 1 x 3 WITH THREE 3d NAILS AT EACH END

ALL (C)

COUNTERBORE 7/8"-DIAMETER HOLES 3/8" DEEP

4" x 1/4" MACHINE BOLTS WITH WASHERS AT EACH END

END VIEW (SECTION)

SLOT & HOLE PLACEMENTS

DRAWING 17-1

Next, using a square, mark and cut the slots in (B), as specified in drawing 17-1 (for more about cutting slots, see page 69). Cut carefully; if the slots are too deep or too shallow, the base won't fit together properly.

Sand or file the slots smooth, then fit the pieces together to check for proper depth of slots.

Now assemble the two halves of the base. To do this, first mark hole placements on the crosspieces, as shown in drawing 17-1. Drill $\frac{7}{8}''$-diameter holes $\frac{3}{8}''$ deep.

Sandwich a leg between two crosspieces, making sure that the ends are flush and that the pieces are positioned at a 90° angle (use a square to check). If you have clamps, clamp the pieces (slide scrap wood under clamps' jaws to protect the soft redwood from

denting).

Centering a $\frac{1}{4}''$ bit in the $\frac{7}{8}''$-diameter holes, drill bolt holes through all three pieces. Put a washer on one bolt, push the bolt through a hole, add another washer, and tighten on a nut. Repeat for all bolt holes. Fit together the two halves to form the complete base (drawing 17-1).

Glue and nail all of the top slats (C) to the perpendicular (C) frame pieces, making sure corners are 90° and keeping all top slats parallel. Then add (D).

Carefully sand the wood, slightly rounding the edges and corners, and apply two coats of clear polyurethane exterior finish.

When the finish dries, set the top on the base to complete your new garden table.

Party Props

For outdoor entertaining

High/Low Tile-top Table

(Photo on facing page)

Durable, multifunctional, and folding: these are the words that best describe this two-level tile-top table. And because it is all of these, it will fill a multitude of needs around the house.

At its low position, place it between a couple of patio chairs or next to your favorite lounge, or display a bonsai or prized plant on it. Or use it at its higher position for serving a small buffet or a candlelight dinner for two. Off-season, either move it indoors or fold it up for minimum-space storage.

When buying tiles for the top, keep in mind that you'll need to modify the dimensions of the table if the tiles are a different size.

Design: Don Rutherford

Tools you'll need:

pencil • measuring tape • square • crosscut saw or power circular saw • coping saw or saber saw • hammer • nailset • drill with a $\frac{1}{16}$'' bit, #10 by 2'' pilot bit, and 1'' power bit • screwdriver • sandpaper and finishing tools. *Helpful tools* include a table saw or radial-arm saw, saber saw, router with a $\frac{1}{4}$''-radius (or smaller) bit, and bar or pipe clamps. *For laying the tile,* you'll need a mastic spreader, grout float or squeegee, large sponge, and several soft cloths.

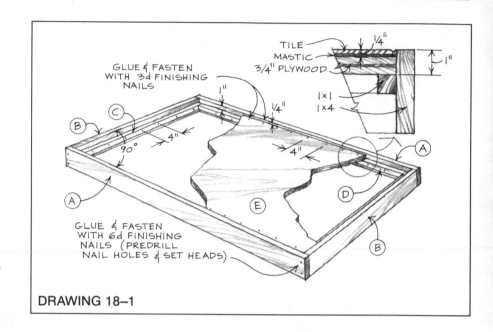

GLUE & FASTEN WITH 3d FINISHING NAILS

TILE
MASTIC
3/4'' PLYWOOD

1×1
1×4

GLUE & FASTEN WITH 6d FINISHING NAILS (PREDRILL NAIL HOLES & SET HEADS)

DRAWING 18—1

Materials list

All hardware and fastenings should be rust-resistant. All redwood should be Clear.
12' of 1 by 4 redwood: 2 @ 6'
16' of 1 by 3 redwood
1' of 1 by 2 redwood
12' of 1 by 1 redwood
2' of 2 by 2 redwood
6' of hardwood doweling, 1'':
  3 @ 2' (be sure they are round and straight)
$\frac{1}{4}$ *sheet of* $\frac{3}{4}$'' fir B-B exterior plywood, 2' by 4'
2 dozen 6d (2'') finishing nails
3 dozen 3d (1$\frac{1}{4}$'') finishing nails
6 flathead screws, 2'' by #10
4 flathead screws, 2$\frac{1}{2}$'' by #10
2 gate hooks, 1$\frac{1}{2}$'', with eye
Waterproof plastic-resin glue
Wood filler (redwood)
Polyurethane penetrating oil-sealer finish
126 glazed ceramic tiles (7 sq. feet), $\frac{1}{4}$'' by 2'' by 4'' (actual size 1$\frac{7}{8}$'' by 3$\frac{7}{8}$'', to allow for a $\frac{1}{8}$'' grout joint)
1 quart of tile mastic (water-resistant)
5 pounds of grout (precolored)
1 pint of grout sealer

Here's How

Cut all of the pieces to size, according to the following cutting list (refer to drawings 18-1, 19-1, and 20-1). Be sure to lay out and check all cuts with a square. For more about cutting, see page 67.

(A) Two 1 by 4s, 43$\frac{5}{8}$''
(B) Two 1 by 4s, 24$\frac{1}{8}$''
(C) Two 1 by 1s, 24$\frac{1}{8}$''
(D) Two 1 by 1s, 40$\frac{5}{8}$''
(E) One $\frac{3}{4}$'' plywood, 24'' by 42''
(F) Four 1 by 3s, 38$\frac{1}{2}$''
(G) One 1 by 3, 21''
(H) Two 1 by 2s, 5''
(I) Two 2 by 2s, 5''
(J) Two 2 by 2s, 4''
(K) One dowel, 1'' by 24''
(L) One dowel, 1'' by 22$\frac{1}{2}$''
(M) One dowel, 1'' by 21''

Note in the detail in drawing 19-1 that the ends of the (F) pieces are rounded. Round them now, using either a coping saw or a saber saw. Also drill the 1''-diameter holes specified in drawing 19-1, keeping the drill bit perpendicular to the surface.

(Continued on page 20)

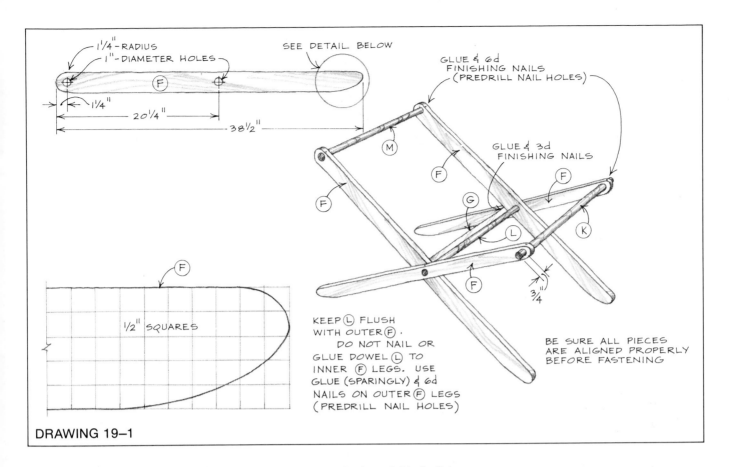

1¼"-RADIUS
1"-DIAMETER HOLES
SEE DETAIL BELOW

F

1¼"
20¼"
38½"

GLUE & 6d
FINISHING NAILS
(PREDRILL NAIL HOLES)

M

GLUE & 3d
FINISHING NAILS

F

F

G

F

L

K

F

3/4"

F

½" SQUARES

KEEP L FLUSH
WITH OUTER F.
DO NOT NAIL OR
GLUE DOWEL L TO
INNER F LEGS. USE
GLUE (SPARINGLY) & 6d
NAILS ON OUTER F LEGS
(PREDRILL NAIL HOLES)

BE SURE ALL PIECES
ARE ALIGNED PROPERLY
BEFORE FASTENING

DRAWING 19—1

Tile-top table, in its highest position, serves as a convenient, portable buffet.

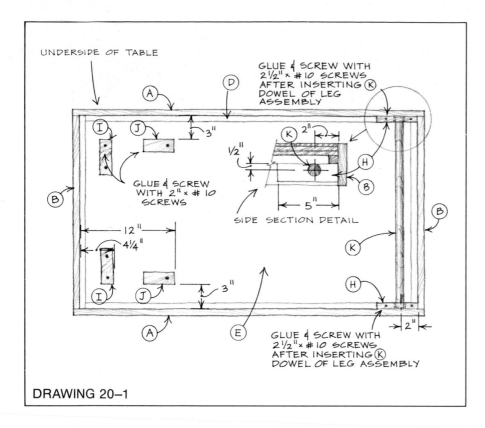

UNDERSIDE OF TABLE

GLUE & SCREW WITH 2½" × #10 SCREWS AFTER INSERTING (K) DOWEL OF LEG ASSEMBLY

GLUE & SCREW WITH 2" × #10 SCREWS

SIDE SECTION DETAIL

GLUE & SCREW WITH 2½" × #10 SCREWS AFTER INSERTING (K) DOWEL OF LEG ASSEMBLY

DRAWING 20–1

dowel (M) and gatehooks into underside of the top to hold legs in place against (I) if you want the table in the low position, or (J) for the high position.

Set all nails, fill the holes, and sand the surfaces. Apply at least two coats of polyurethane penetrating oil-sealer finish. (It's best to apply several coats to the frame pieces (A) and (B) so that the grout will not stain the wood.) Let the finish dry thoroughly.

Spread tile mastic on the plywood top, using a notched spreader as specified by label directions. Starting at one corner, lay sheets of tile in position so that the spacing between sheets is the same as the spacing between individual tiles. If any of the tiles are misaligned, cut through the mesh surrounding them with a utility knife and slide them into proper position.

After the tiles are in place, embed them in the mastic by sliding a piece of ¾" plywood over the tiled surface and tapping it with a hammer. Remove any excess mastic from the tiles and grooves. Allow to dry thoroughly.

Mix grout according to label directions. Its consistency should be similar to thick mayonnaise. Proceed by the following steps:

1) Spread the grout over the tiles, using a rubber float, squeegee, or sponge. Work the grout into the joints until they are packed and free of voids and air pockets.

2) Remove the excess grout, working diagonally across the joints.

3) Soak a clean sponge in clear water and wring out. Wipe off as much of the remaining grout as possible. Work the joints until they are smooth, rinsing the sponge frequently in clear water.

4) Allow any grout remaining on tiles to dry to a haze (about 30 minutes). Rub it off with a soft cloth.

5) Cover the grouted top with damp cloths for about 24 hours, to let the grout cure.

6) After the grout is fully cured (about 2 weeks), apply the sealer recommended by your tile and grout supplier.

. . . Continued from page 18

Round off the edges of the (A) and (B) pieces and the edges and ends of the (F) and (G) pieces, using sandpaper or a router. Also sand and apply two coats of polyurethane finish to the (F) and (G) pieces (it's easiest to do this prior to assembly).

See drawings 18-1 and 19-1 for proper construction of the box-frame tabletop and the leg assembly. Assemble the tabletop, following drawing 18-1. Use waterproof glue and the nails specified. It's easiest to fasten (D) to (A), and (C) to (B) before joining the frame pieces (A) and (B). Add the plywood top (E) last.

Next put together the leg assembly, according to drawing 19-1, working on a flat surface. Before joining anything permanently, check the fit of the dowels in the 1"-diameter holes. If necessary, sand the inside surfaces of the holes. The pivot points between dowel (L) and the inside (F) legs must allow free movement. If they don't, apply a little paste wax to the inside surfaces of the holes.

Assemble the inside (F) legs with the 1 by 2 (G), dowel (L), and dowel (M) first, keeping the ends of (M) and (G) flush with the outer faces of the legs (F). Remember to predrill holes ($\frac{1}{16}$" bit) for the 6d nails. Be sure the legs (F) are parallel and the (M), (L), and (G) pieces are perpendicular to them. Note that dowel (L) protrudes ¾" beyond the inner leg (F) at both ends and is not fastened.

Add the outer legs (F) and fasten to the dowels (L) and (K) as specified. Use the glue sparingly so you don't accidentally glue the legs where they should be pivoting.

While the glue dries, drill the 1"-diameter holes in the pivoting blocks (H) and the pilot holes for fastening these in place (see drawing 20-1). Then slip the pivoting blocks (H) over the ends of the (K) dowel and glue and screw the pivoting blocks (H) to the underside of (E) with 2½" by #10 screws, countersinking the screws. Check the pivoting action of leg assembly before gluing. If the legs don't pivot freely, without binding, sand the inner faces of (H).

Round off the edges of blocks (I) and (J) nearest left side in drawing above and glue and screw them in place, where specified in drawing 20-1 (drill pilot holes for the screws). Drill $\frac{1}{16}$" holes and install screw eye into

Mexican Sunshades

With glowing colors above and cool shade below, these simple sun-shades can make garden galas more festive and more comfortable. The design is borrowed from shades in a Mexican marketplace. The originals are simply crude lumber and white canvas; these use stock milled lumber bolted together and covered with brightly colored fabric.

Some machine sewing is required, but it's not complicated, and since the shade ends up high in the bright sky, expert tailoring isn't needed.
Design: Rick Morrall

Tools you'll need:

pencil · measuring tape · square · crosscut saw or power circular saw · drill with a $\frac{5}{16}''$ bit · hammer · pliers · sewing equipment and a sewing machine.

Materials list (for one)

All hardware and fastenings should be rust-resistant.
20' of 1 by 2 fir: 2 @ 10'
10' of 2 by 2 fir (or a 10-foot "tree stake")
1' of 3''-diameter steel pipe, with cap
2 carriage bolts, $\frac{5}{16}''$ by $2\frac{1}{2}''$, with washers and wing nuts
Half dozen 10d (3'') box nails
Waterproof resorcinol glue
4 long decorative upholstery tacks
5 yards of 45''-wide cotton or polyester/cotton fabric (choose translucent fabric); for a patchwork-square effect, buy $2\frac{1}{2}$ yards in each of two colors or patterns
Matching cotton-wrapped polyester thread

Here's How

First, cut the fabric in half crosswise and sew the two 90''-long pieces together to make a square (or form a patchwork pattern by piecing

As party shades, these festive shelters create a colorful oasis under the sun.

different fabrics together). Along each edge, fold about an inch over twice and hem so the finished shade is 85'' square. To reinforce corners, resew where the hems overlap.

Next, cut the 2 by 2 about 9' long. Drill a $\frac{5}{16}''$ hole through the center of the 2 by 2 post, 3'' from the top. Turn the post 90° and drill another hole $1\frac{1}{2}''$ lower than the first.

On a wide side of each 1 by 2, mark the center point, then drill a $\frac{5}{16}''$ hole an inch to one side of the mark; when the two 1 by 2s are bolted to the 2 by 2 post, they should overlap at their centers.

To keep crosspieces from blowing

into a vertical position, glue and nail a 3''-long 1 by 2 scrap block about 1'' below each hole on the post. Attach crosspieces to the post with bolts, washers, and wing nuts; tighten with pliers.

Embed the 3''-diameter pipe (cap down) in the lawn and place the post in it.

Finally, drape the fabric over the crosspieces and secure with one long upholstery tack at each corner. Tilt the shades as you wish. Gentle breezes will cause the fabric to billow and relax gracefully, and if everything is secure, the shades should withstand even strong winds.

Rustic Dining Set

Old World charm from rough redwood

Trestle Table

Bold, rugged style and simple construction are the marks of this handsome outdoor table that you can build in a weekend.

The table gets its rustic character from the rough-sawn redwood lumber it's made from. Because this grade of lumber is not normally kiln-dried, be careful to select pieces that are as straight as possible. Store the wood flat, off the ground, and allow it to dry out for about two months (if you're in a hurry, you can substitute kiln-dried, surfaced wood).

Also, when you buy the lumber check the dimensions for consistency. The measurements given for the table are based on lumber exactly 2″ thick. If your lumber's dimensions differ, you'll need to make the appropriate changes in construction.

Design: Scott Fitzgerrell

Tools you'll need:

pencil · measuring tape · square · crosscut saw or power circular saw · saber saw or keyhole saw · rasp · drill with $\frac{3}{8}$″ and $\frac{7}{8}$″ bits · socket wrench with a $\frac{1}{2}$″ socket · adjustable wrench or pliers · rough sandpaper and finishing tools. *Helpful tools* include a table saw or radial-arm saw, drill press, band saw, and power sander.

Bold and simple dining set consists of trestle table, benches, and sideboard.

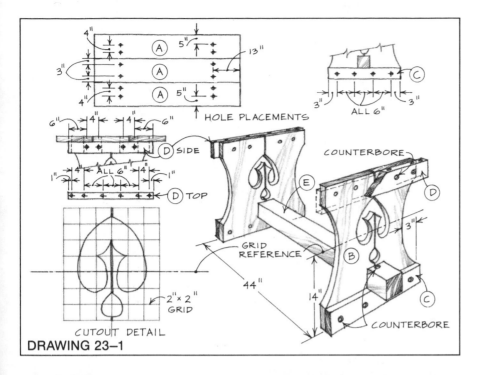

HOLE PLACEMENTS

ALL 6"

D SIDE

D TOP

COUNTERBORE

GRID REFERENCE

44"

14"

13"

3"

COUNTERBORE

2" x 2" GRID

CUTOUT DETAIL

DRAWING 23–1

use either a band saw, saber saw, or keyhole saw. Of course, the band saw is by far the easiest; if you're using one of the other saws, you'll also need patience and a coarse blade. Some of the tight curves are easiest to make by first drilling with a $\frac{7}{8}$" spade bit, then finishing with a saw or coarse rasp.

If you don't have the necessary tools or patience, consider marking the curves and taking the wood to a cabinetmaker to be cut.

Begin assembly by laying the four end halves (B) in pairs on a flat surface. Position the top and bottom tie pieces (C) and (D) on them and mark the bolt hole locations on the tie pieces.

Counterbore $\frac{7}{8}$"-diameter holes $\frac{3}{8}$" deep for washers and nuts. Then center a $\frac{3}{8}$" bit in each of those holes and drill through for the bolts. Push washers onto the $3\frac{1}{2}$" bolts, push the bolts through from the other sides of the (B) pieces, add a washer to each, and tighten on the nuts with a $\frac{1}{2}$" socket wrench.

Stand the joined end pieces up and push the 4 by 4 (E) through the square holes; then counterbore, drill, and assemble it to (C), using $7\frac{1}{2}$" bolts.

Center the top boards, best side up, across the tie pieces (D). Be sure all (A) boards are flush along both ends. Counterbore and drill bolt holes where shown in drawing 23-1. Also counterbore from the undersides of the (D) pieces. Put washers on the $5\frac{1}{2}$" bolts, push them through from the top, add washers, and tighten on nuts, using a socket wrench and $\frac{1}{2}$" socket.

Finish the table with two or three coats of polyurethane penetrating oil-sealer.

Materials list

All hardware and fastenings should be rust-resistant.

30' of 2 by 12 rough redwood:
  5 @ 6'
6' of 4 by 4 rough redwood
12' of 2 by 4 rough redwood:
  2 @ 6'
2 machine bolts, $\frac{5}{16}$" by $7\frac{1}{2}$"
12 machine bolts, $\frac{5}{16}$" by $5\frac{1}{2}$"
16 machine bolts, $\frac{5}{16}$" by $3\frac{1}{2}$"
30 nuts, $\frac{5}{16}$"
60 washers, $\frac{5}{16}$"
Polyurethane penetrating oil-sealer finish

Here's How

Measure, mark, and cut the lengths you'll need from the lumber. The following cutting list gives the proper lengths. Use a square for marking and checking your cuts.

(A) Three 2 by 12s, 6'
(B) Four 2 by 12s, 26"
(C) Two 2 by 4s, 24"
(D) Two 2 by 4s, 28"
(E) One 4 by 4, 52"

After cutting, thoroughly sand all pieces. Remove the burrs and splinters, but don't remove the mill marks and scars that give the wood its rustic character.

Make a paper or carboard pattern of the cut-out design for the end pieces, according to drawing 23-1. Use this as a template for marking the end pieces (B). Also mark a square hole for (E).

For cutting these curves, you can

Trestle Benches

(Photo on facing page)

Though these benches were designed to accompany the table they're shown with on page 22, they provide very handsome, sturdy seating on their own.

Much of the information given in the directions for the table applies to the benches as well; be sure to read those directions before building the benches.

Design: Scott Fitzgerrell

Tools you'll need:

pencil · measuring tape · square · crosscut saw or power circular saw · saber saw or keyhole saw · rasp · drill with $\frac{3}{16}$", $\frac{1}{4}$", $\frac{3}{8}$", and $\frac{7}{8}$" bits · bench vise · socket wrench with $\frac{7}{16}$" and $\frac{1}{2}$" sockets · adjustable wrench or pliers · rough sandpaper and finishing tools. *Helpful tools* include a table saw or radial-arm saw, drill press, band saw, and power sander.

(Continued on next page)

. . . *Continued from page 23*

Materials list (for one bench):

All hardware and fastenings should be rust-resistant.

18′ of 2 by 6 rough redwood:
   3 @ 6′
10′ of 2 by 2 rough redwood
1 dozen 8d (2½″) finishing nails
20 machine bolts, $\frac{5}{16}$″ by 3½″
40 washers, $\frac{5}{16}$″
20 nuts, $\frac{5}{16}$″
2 carriage bolts, ¼″ by 2½″
1 lag screw, ¼″ by 1¼″
2 nuts, ¼″
3 washers, ¼″
1 metal mending plate, ¾″ by 6″
Polyurethane penetrating oil-sealer finish

Here's How

Begin by measuring and cutting the lengths you'll need, according to the following list (refer to drawing 24-1). Use a square for marking and checking all cuts. To make two benches, double the quantities.

(A) Two 2 by 6s, 6′
(B) Four 2 by 6s, 16″
(C) Five 2 by 2s, 12″
(D) Two 2 by 2s, approximately 30″ (measure and cut later)

Also bevel the corners of two of the tie pieces (C), as detailed in drawing 24-1.

Follow the directions given for the rustic table regarding sanding, cutting the end pieces, and joining the end pieces (use 3½″ bolts). Refer to drawing 24-2 for the cut-out design pattern.

Counterbore and bolt the seat boards (A) to three of the tie pieces (C), using 3½″ bolts.

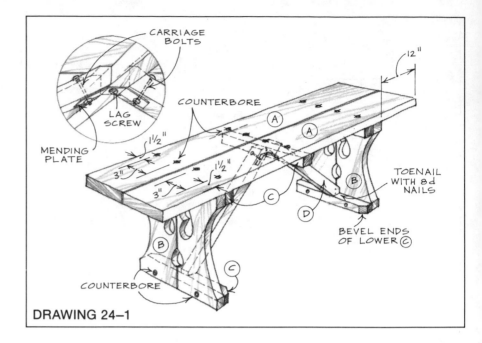

DRAWING 24—1

Turn the bench on its side and lay the 2 by 2 braces (D) across the central and lower trestle tie pieces (C). Mark on (D) the angles of intersection, and cut the braces (D) at these angles (see drawing 24-1).

Put the mending plate in a vise and bend it to the proper angle for joining the braces (see the detail in drawing 24-1). Hold it in place on the braces and mark for bolt holes in mending plate. Drill ¼″ holes for the carriage bolts and a $\frac{3}{16}$″ hole for the lag screw. Insert the bolts and lag screw. Toenail lower ends of (D) to (C) and (B).

Finish with two or three coats of polyurethane oil-sealer.

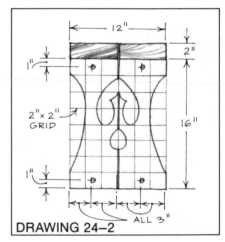

DRAWING 24—2

Rustic Sideboard

(Photo on page 22)

With plenty of counter space for serving buffet-style or for barbecuing, this open sideboard is the ideal complement for the table and bench accompanying it in the photograph on page 22. It has the same rustic charm, easy construction, and durability.

It is boldly designed from standard sizes of rough-sawn redwood lumber. Joinery is simple—pieces are just bolted or screwed together.

Be sure to let the lumber season (dry) before cutting it.

Design: Scott Fitzgerrell

Tools you'll need:

pencil • measuring tape • square • crosscut saw or power circular saw • saber saw or keyhole saw • rasp • drill with $\frac{3}{8}$″ and $\frac{7}{8}$″ bits and a #8 by 2½″ pilot bit • hammer • socket wrench with a ½″ socket • screwdriver • rough sandpaper and finishing tools. *Helpful tools* include a table saw or radial-arm saw, drill press, band saw, and power sander.

Materials list

All hardware and fastenings should be rust-resistant.

36' of 2 by 12 rough redwood:
  6 @ 6'
24' of 1 by 12 rough redwood:
  4 @ 6'
8' of 2 by 4 rough redwood
12' of 2 by 2 rough redwood:
  2 @ 6'
16 machine bolts, $5\frac{1}{2}$'' by $\frac{5}{16}$''
16 machine bolts, $3\frac{1}{2}$'' by $\frac{5}{16}$''
32 nuts, $\frac{5}{16}$''
64 washers, $\frac{5}{16}$''
1 pound of 16d ($3\frac{1}{2}$'') common nails
36 flathead screws, $2\frac{1}{2}$'' by #8
Polyurethane penetrating oil-sealer finish

Here's How

Begin by cutting the lumber to the lengths you'll need, according to the following cutting schedule (refer to drawing 25-1). Use a square for marking and checking your cuts. For more about cutting, see page 67.

Keep in mind that the dimensions given are based on lumber having a standard thickness of 2''. If your lumber's actual thickness differs from this, you'll have to change dimensions accordingly.

(A) Two 2 by 12s, 6'
(B) Two 2 by 12s, 5'
(C) Four 2 by 12s, 3'
(D) Four 2 by 4s, 2'
(E) One 1 by 12, 5'
(F) One 1 by 12, 1'
(G) Six 1 by 12s, approximately 30'' (measure and cut later)
(H) Two 2 by 2s, 5'
(I) Two 2 by 2s, 1'

For information on sanding the pieces, making the cutouts, and joining the end pieces (C), refer to the rustic table directions on page 23. Drawing 25-2 shows the shapes to cut out for the buffet's end pieces (C).

Also draw and cut a curve along the front edges of two of the end boards (C), as shown in drawing 25-2, leaving 4'' of the straight edge at the top and 6'' at bottom. Make the narrowest point about one third of the way down from the top. (You can use one of these pieces as a pattern for marking its mate.)

Assembly is fairly simple. Lay the two pieces for each end (C) on a flat surface, positioned as shown in drawing 25-2. Bolt the tie pieces (D) in place with $3\frac{1}{2}$'' bolts, using the same methods described for the table base (see page 23).

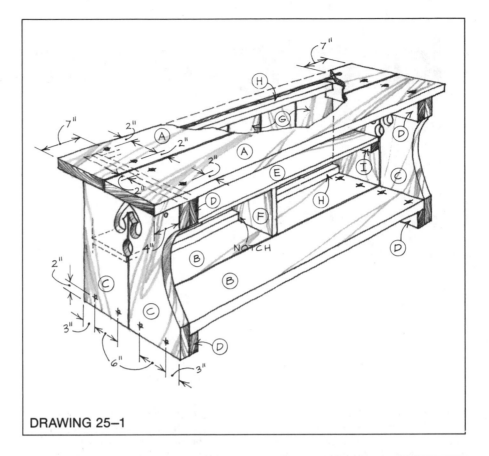

DRAWING 25—1

For the next step, you may need a helper. Hold the end pieces upright and place two (B) shelves side by side on the lower tie pieces (D). Mark bolt hole locations on the tops of the shelves (B). Counterbore $\frac{1}{2}$'' deep with a $\frac{7}{8}$'' bit and drill $\frac{3}{8}$'' bolt holes. Assemble with $\frac{5}{16}$'' by $5\frac{1}{2}$'' bolts, washers, and nuts.

Set the top boards (A) in place so they are square with each other and overhang (C) by 4'' at each end. Counterbore, then drill $\frac{3}{8}$'' holes through (A) and (D). Counterbore holes from bottom of (D) too. Bolt in place with $5\frac{1}{2}$'' bolts, washers, and nuts.

Measure the distance between the top (A) and bottom (B) boards and cut the (G) pieces to that length. Nail a 2 by 2 (H) 1'' in from the back, to both the top of (B) and the bottom of (A), using 16d nails. Then screw the five outer 1 by 12s (G) to these (H) pieces, after first drilling three pilot holes for the $2\frac{1}{2}$'' by #8 screws at each end of each board.

Rip the remaining 1 by 12, if necessary, to make it fit the gap left after the first five were attached, and screw it in place.

For the interior shelf (E), nail cleats (I) in place with 16d nails. Notch the 1 by 12 (F) to fit around

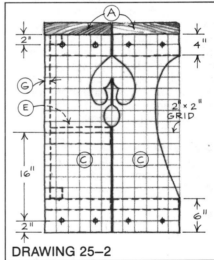

DRAWING 25—2

the lower 2 by 2 (H) and nail it in place through (B), (E), and (G) to support the middle of the interior shelf (E). Nail ends of (E) to (I).

If necessary, sand the pieces a bit more to round off corners and edges. Finish with two or three coats of polyurethane penetrating oil-sealer.

Hanging Furniture

The height of free-swinging comfort

Canvas and Plastic Pipe Hammock

(Photo on facing page)

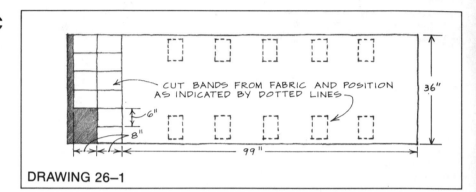

CUT BANDS FROM FABRIC AND POSITION AS INDICATED BY DOTTED LINES

36"

6"

8"

99"

DRAWING 26-1

You can make this hammock in one afternoon and spend hundreds of future afternoons enjoying the fruits of your labor. Gathering the materials is the most time-consuming task. You'll need to visit an awning maker to get the canvas; a ship chandlery to get dacron thread and rope; a plumbing supply store for steel pipe, plastic pipe, and PVC solvent; and a hardware store for the hammock hanging materials.
Design: Lynne Morrall

Tools you'll need:
pencil · measuring tape · hacksaw · sewing equipment and a sewing machine with a heavy-duty needle.

Materials list
All hardware and fastenings should be rust-resistant.
$3\frac{1}{4}$ yards of 36"-wide #8 canvas
Matching dacron thread
20' of 40-gauge rigid PVC plastic pipe, 1" (white)
4 PVC 90° elbows, 1"
1 pint can of PVC solvent
20' of steel pipe, $\frac{1}{2}$"
Enough $\frac{1}{2}$" dacron rope to hang the hammock
2 swivel snaps, $\frac{7}{8}$"

Here's How
Make the canvas sling first. Cut out the main body and ten bands, as diagrammed in drawing 26-1.

Equip your sewing machine with a heavy-duty needle. For all seams (except the narrow hems on the sides of the sling and on the bands) make several rows of stitching for strength. Backstitch to secure the ends of all seams.

Hem the long edges of the main fabric body by folding under $\frac{1}{4}$", then folding under another $\frac{3}{8}$" and pinning. Stitch through the resulting triple thickness.

Turn under $\frac{1}{2}$" of one end of the main hammock body and stitch once; fold under $3\frac{1}{2}$" and topstitch in place. Repeat at the other end of the main hammock body. Then turn under $\frac{1}{4}$" and hem the long edges of the bands.

Turn the main hammock body upside down. Beginning about 7" from each looped hammock end, space five bands (wrong side up) evenly along each long edge of the hammock, as shown in drawing 26-1. The bands should be about a foot apart. Pin the bands in place, or mark their positions with a pencil.

Attach one band to the hammock with a single seam $\frac{1}{4}$" from the end of the band near the hammock's long edge. Fold the band along that seam out over the hammock's edge and make several rows of topstitching near the fold. Now turn the hammock right side up. Fold under and stitch a $\frac{1}{4}$" hem on the free end of the band. Pin that end of the band to

the right side of the fabric about 2" from the hammock's edge, forming a loop. Secure to the hammock with several rows of topstitching. Repeat for all the bands.

If any of the stitching pulls out after the hammock is assembled, a sail repair kit from a ship chandlery can be used to resew the fabric pieces by hand.

Next make the frame. With a hacksaw, cut both the metal and plastic pipes into two 7' lengths and two 3' lengths. Slide the metal pipe inside the plastic pipe. Then slip the pipes through the fabric loops.

Cover the floor with papers to protect against dripping solvent as you assemble the hammock frame. Also be careful not to spill solvent on the fabric. Starting at one corner, apply solvent to the elbow and pipes—following label directions—and quickly assemble. Repeat on all the corners, making sure the elbows and pipes lie flat on the floor as you glue them. Leave undisturbed for the recommended setting time.

The hammock in the photograph on page 27 is suspended with heavy dacron rope and swivel snaps. Just tie the rope to the corners of the hammock frame (you can fuse the free ends of the rope with a candle flame to prevent raveling).

Canvas and Plastic Pipe Hammock (see facing page)

Porch Swing

(Photo on page 29)

Maybe it's the fresh air and the soft breezes. Or maybe it's the feeling of gently swaying back and forth. For one reason or another, porch swings are fun for kids, relaxing for adults, and romantic for couples.

If you like the idea of having your own porch swing, consider this one. More than large enough for two people, it's particularly comfortable—even without cushions— because its back pivots to the angle that's most comfortable for your back.

What's more, you can build it in a weekend from stock sizes of lumber, using glue, nails, and bolts for joinery.
Design: Don Vandervort

Tools you'll need:

pencil · measuring tape · compass · square · crosscut saw · coping saw or saber saw · drill with $\frac{5}{32}''$, $\frac{1}{4}''$, $\frac{5}{16}''$, and $\frac{3}{4}''$ bits · chisel · hammer · nail-set · socket wrench with a $\frac{7}{16}''$ socket · sandpaper and finishing tools. *Helpful tools* include C-clamps; bench vise; power circular saw, table saw, or radial-arm saw; drill press; and power sander.

Materials list

All hardware and fastenings should
  be rust-resistant. All redwood
  should be Clear.
38' of 1 by 6 redwood: 1 @ 10',
  2 @ 8', 2 @ 6'
4' of 1 by 4 redwood
16' of 2 by 3 redwood: 2 @ 8'
16' of 2 by 2 redwood: 2 @ 8'
1 dozen 10d (3'') finishing nails
1 pound of 6d (2'') finishing nails
2 dozen 4d (1½'') finishing nails
4 lag screws, $\frac{1}{4}''$ by 5'', with washers
2 machine bolts, $\frac{1}{4}''$ by 5'', with nuts
10 washers, $\frac{1}{4}''$
4 eyebolts, $\frac{5}{16}''$ by 4'', with washers
  and nuts
4 "hammock hooks" or $\frac{5}{16}''$ by 4''
  screw hooks
Enough $\frac{3}{16}''$ vinyl-coated, stranded
  cable for hanging the swing

16 wire rope clamps, 8 thimbles, $\frac{3}{16}''$
Waterproof resorcinol glue
Wood filler (redwood/cedar)
Clear polyurethane exterior finish

Here's How

Begin by cutting the various pieces to length, according to the following cutting list. Also refer to drawing 28-1. Be sure to use a square for marking and checking all cuts. For more about cutting, see page 67.

Cut all (A) and (B) from the 10'-long 1 by 6, all (H) from the 8-footers, and all (K) from the 6-footers. Cut all (C) and (G) from one 8-foot 2 by 3, and both (F) from the other. Cut all (D) and (J) from one 8-foot 2 by 2, and both (I) from the other. And cut both (E) from the 1 by 4. As you cut them, label the pieces for easy identification.

(A) Four 1 by 6s, 14¼''
(B) Four 1 by 6s, 12''
(C) Two 2 by 3s, 24¾''
(D) Two 2 by 2s, 23⅞''
(E) Two 1 by 4s, 23⅞''
(F) Two 2 by 3s, 47⅛''
(G) Two 2 by 3s, 20½''
(H) Eight 1 by 6s, 21¼''
(I)   Two 2 by 2s, 43⅝''
(J) Two 2 by 2s, 15''
(K) Eight 1 by 6s, 17''

(Continued on next page)

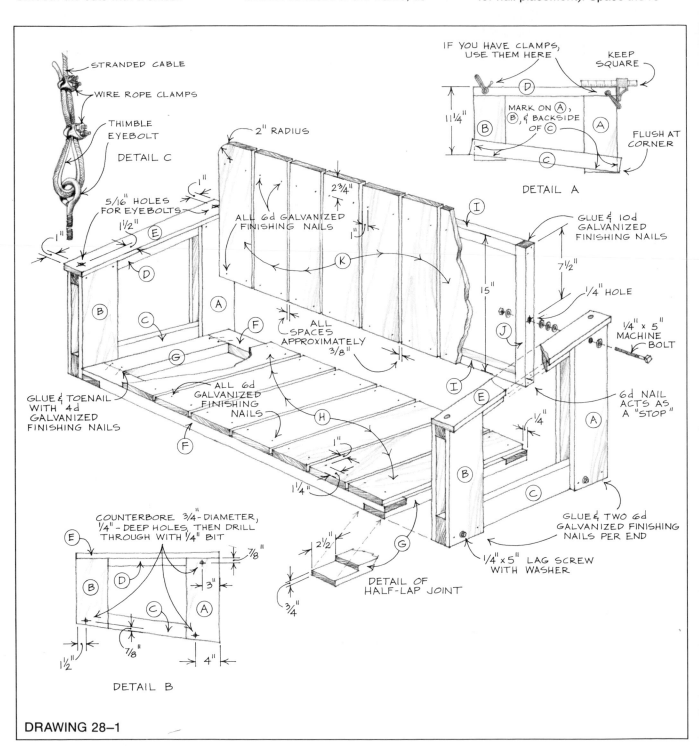

. . . Continued from page 27

Now lay out one each of pieces (A), (B), (C), and (D) for one side assembly, as shown in detail A.

Cut these (A), (B), and (C) pieces, then use them as templates for marking and cutting the other (A), (B), and (C) pieces.

While you're marking and cutting, mark and cut the half-lap corner joints with a crosscut saw in (F) and (G), as detailed in drawing 28-1. Smooth the cuts with a chisel.

Now it's time to begin the assembly process. Start with the side frames. Glue and nail together with 6d finishing nails the (A), (B), (C), and (D) pieces, according to drawing 28-1. Be sure to keep all pieces flush along their edges and ends.

Next assemble the seat frame. Glue the joints, check for square, and toenail with 4d finishing nails—two at each joint from both top and bottom surfaces of the frame, as

shown in the drawing.

Lay the frame right side up on a flat work surface—the floor will do. Gather together all of the (H) boards and arrange them for color and grain pattern as you prefer. Be sure the best sides of the boards face upward.

Using 6d finishing nails (two at each end), nail the two end boards in place, spaced ¼″ in from the ends of the seat frame (see drawing 28-1 for nail placement). Space the re-

STRANDED CABLE

WIRE ROPE CLAMPS

THIMBLE EYEBOLT

DETAIL C

5/16″ HOLES FOR EYEBOLTS

1½″

1″

2″ RADIUS

ALL 6d GALVANIZED FINISHING NAILS

2¾″

1″

ALL SPACES APPROXIMATELY 3/8″

15″

IF YOU HAVE CLAMPS, USE THEM HERE

KEEP SQUARE

MARK ON (A), (B), & BACKSIDE OF (C)

FLUSH AT CORNER

11¼″

DETAIL A

GLUE & 10d GALVANIZED FINISHING NAILS

7½″

¼″ HOLE

¼″ × 5″ MACHINE BOLT

6d NAIL ACTS AS A "STOP"

GLUE & TOENAIL WITH 4d GALVANIZED FINISHING NAILS

ALL 6d GALVANIZED FINISHING NAILS

1″

1¼″

¼″

¼″

GLUE & TWO 6d GALVANIZED FINISHING NAILS PER END

¼″ × 5″ LAG SCREW WITH WASHER

COUNTERBORE ¾″-DIAMETER, ¼″-DEEP HOLES, THEN DRILL THROUGH WITH ¼″ BIT

7/8″

3″

7/8″

1½″

4″

DETAIL B

2½″

¾″

DETAIL OF HALF-LAP JOINT

DRAWING 28–1

28 Porch Swing

maining (H) boards evenly (with about $\frac{3}{8}''$ separation) between the two end boards, and nail them in place, keeping the ends flush with the front edge of the frame.

Now make the back frame. Glue and nail together with 10d finishing nails the (I) and (J) pieces, and check for square.

Lay out, arrange, and fasten the (K) boards, using the same methods as for the seat. Mark the top out-side corner of each of the end boards with a compass set at a 2'' radius, and trim, using a saber saw or coping saw.

Now you're ready to join the side frames to the seat and back. In (A) and (B), counterbore $\frac{3}{4}''$-diameter holes $\frac{1}{4}''$ deep at the locations shown in detail B. Keep in mind that at this stage the two side frames will be mirror images of each other—drill the holes from opposite sides.

Center a $\frac{1}{4}''$ bit in each of these counterbored holes and drill through. Be sure to drill straight (for more about drilling, see page 70). Also drill the $\frac{1}{4}''$ hole through (J).

Now set the seat platform on a flat workbench or table. Place one end of the seat platform about 3'' in from the table's edge. Set the proper side frame upright against the seat plat-form, positioned as shown in draw-ing 28-1.

Mark for pilot holes in the seat by re-drilling through the holes in the side with a $\frac{1}{4}''$ bit, then remove the side frame. Drill $\frac{5}{32}''$ holes about $1\frac{1}{2}''$ deep at these two locations. Again, be sure to drill straight.

Turn the seat around and repeat for the other side.

Push a washer onto each lag screw and screw the side frames to the base.

Next, attach the back to the two side frames. It is held only by two $\frac{1}{4}''$ by 5'' machine bolts—for each bolt, there are washers under both the head and the nut and three washers between the back and side frames. By tightening these nuts, you can keep the back from swivel-ing out of the upright position on its own. Add a 6d nail in (J) where shown, letting it protrude about $\frac{3}{4}''$. This will act as a "stop," keep-ing the backrest in relative position. Glue and nail the arms (E) onto the side frames; use 6d finishing nails.

Set all exposed nails, fill nail holes, and sand the pieces until they are smooth and the edges are slightly rounded. Wipe clean and apply two coats of clear exterior polyurethane finish. Allow to dry.

Drill $\frac{5}{16}''$ holes in the tops of the arms for eyebolts. Push eyebolts through, add washers, and tighten on nuts.

Decide where you plan to hang the swing (hang it only from a sturdy beam, joist, or tree limb), then measure and cut the cables. For each cable, determine the length you'll need to suspend the seat approximately 16'' off the ground, and allow two feet extra.

Attach hooks securely to the sup-porting beam, joist, or tree limb, then form a loop at one end of each cable to slip over the hooks. (Refer to detail C for proper assembly of wire rope clamps and thimbles.) Thread the other ends of the cables through clamps, thimbles, and eyebolts to hang the swing, making any adjust-ments needed to ensure that the swing's arms will hang in a level position.

Porch swing is fun for everyone. Its back pivots for comfort.

Pine Patio Group

Easy chair, windscreen, coffee table

Casual Chair

During the summer months, this pine chair can be the highlight of your outdoor living. Not only will it brighten up your yard or patio, it'll also offer you hours of leisurely comfort.

And when bad weather sets in, your chair needn't be banished to storage. Because it doesn't have the "heavy" or "bulky" design of some other outdoor furniture, it looks great indoors too!

The chair is made from stock sizes of lumber, joined by glue and nails.

Design: Donald Wm. MacDonald

Tools you'll need:

pencil · measuring tape · square · crosscut saw or power circular saw · hammer · nailset (or large nail) · C-clamps · sandpaper and finishing tools · sewing equipment and a sewing machine with a heavy-duty needle. *Helpful tools* include a table saw or radial-arm saw and a power sander.

A repeated pattern of 1 by 2s is the design element that accents this patio grouping.

Materials list

All hardware and fastenings should be rust-resistant.

14' by 2 by 2 Clear pine (or equivalent)

50' of 1 by 2 Clear pine (or equivalent): 1 @ 10', 5 @ 8'

$\frac{1}{8}$ sheet of $\frac{3}{4}$" A-C exterior birch plywood, 2' by 2'

1 pound of 6d (2") finishing nails

1 dozen 8d (2$\frac{1}{4}$") finishing nails

Waterproof resorcinol glue

Wood filler (pine)

Polyurethane penetrating oil-sealer finish

1$\frac{1}{3}$ yards of 36"-wide #6 canvas

Matching cotton-wrapped polyester thread

17" by 22$\frac{1}{2}$" of 2"-thick foam

Here's How

Cut all wood pieces to size, according to the following cutting list (refer to drawing 31-1). Be sure to use a square for marking and checking all cuts. For more about cutting, see page 67. Cut (A) through (E) from the 2 by 2 stock. Cut all of (F) from one 8'-long 1 by 2, all of (G) from another, all of (H) from two 8'-long 1 by 2s, three of (I) from another, and four of (I) from the 10-footer.

(A) Two 2 by 2s, 15"

(B) Two 2 by 2s, 25"

(C) and (D) Two 2 by 2s, 22$\frac{1}{4}$"

(E) One 2 by 2, 23$\frac{3}{4}$"

(F) Four 1 by 2s, 23$\frac{3}{4}$"

(G) Four 1 by 2s, 22$\frac{1}{4}$"

(H) Eight 1 by 2s, 23$\frac{3}{4}$"

(I) Seven 1 by 2s, 29$\frac{1}{2}$"

(J) One $\frac{3}{4}$" birch plywood, 17" by 22$\frac{1}{4}$"

Once you've done the basic cutting, you're ready to glue and nail the pieces together. Use waterproof glue at all joints, then secure with finishing nails. For nailing the 1 by 2s, use 6d finishing nails; for the 2 by 2s, use 8d (two nails per joint).

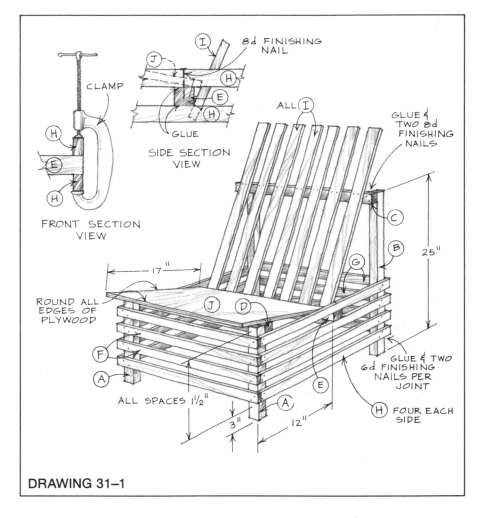

DRAWING 31-1

Begin the assembly by fastening the four front 1 by 2 slats (F) to the two front legs (A) as shown in drawing 31-1. They should overlap the legs by $\frac{3}{4}$" to meet the side slats (H). You can use a 1 by 2, placed flat, to gauge spacing between the slats. To the other side of the front legs (A), fasten (D), square and flush with the ends of (A).

Next make the back leg assembly by fastening the top two and the bottom 1 by 2 slats (G) to the back legs (B). Leave off the fourth slat to simplify nailing the seat back slats (I). The ends of slats (G) should be flush with the outside of the back legs (B). Then fasten the 2 by 2 (C) in place at the top of the back legs.

Connect the front and back leg assemblies with the side slats (H), as shown in drawing 31-1. Be sure that (E) will fit between the two top slats.

Now check to be sure the frame sits evenly on the floor. If it doesn't, trim one or two legs slightly.

Fasten (E) between the top two side slats (H), as detailed in drawing 31-1. To do this, glue the pieces, carefully drive an 8d nail down through each top slat (H) into (E), and clamp the pieces together until the glue dries. Nail on the seat (J) and the back slats (I). Fasten the seat (J) to (E) and (D) with 6d nails, then fasten the back slats (I) to (C) and (E). Finally, fasten the fourth back slat (G) to the back legs (B).

Set all nails and fill the holes. Sand and finish with three coats of polyurethane penetrating oil-sealer.

You can make the 17" by 22$\frac{1}{2}$" by 2" box-type cushion by following directions on page 78, or have it made at an upholstery shop.

Pine and Acrylic Windscreen

(Photo on page 30)

Both elegant and simple, this screen of pine and acrylic plastic can warm up a chilly corner fast. It blocks the wind, yet allows a maximum of light and warmth to penetrate. Or, if you prefer privacy, you can substitute opaque or tinted panels when you make the screen.

Though the screen we show has three panels, you can make yours any length—it's designed as single-panel modules, so you can make any number you want.

Design: Donald Wm. MacDonald

Tools you'll need:

pencil · grease pencil · measuring tape · compass · square · crosscut saw or power circular saw · coping saw · rasp or file · drill with $\frac{1}{4}''$ and $\frac{7}{32}''$ bits and a #10 by $1\frac{1}{2}''$ pilot bit · hammer · nailset (or large nail) · sandpaper and finishing tools. *Helpful tools* include a table saw or radial-arm saw, drill press, and power sander.

Materials list (for three panels)

All hardware and fastenings should be rust-resistant.
98' of 1 by 2 Clear pine (or equivalent): 5 @ 10', 6 @ 8'
4 carriage bolts, 3'' by $\frac{1}{4}''$
30 flathead screws, $1\frac{1}{2}''$ by #10
1 pound of 3d ($1\frac{1}{4}''$) finishing nails
Waterproof resorcinol glue
Wood filler (pine)
3 sheets of acrylic plastic, $\frac{1}{8}''$ by 24'' by 46''
Polyurethane penetrating oil-sealer finish

Here's How

Begin by cutting the 1 by 2s to length. From the 10-footers, cut twenty pieces 28'' long; from the 8-footers, cut twelve pieces 48'' long. Be sure to use a square for marking and checking your cuts. For more about techniques for cutting, see page 67.

Next, drill $\frac{1}{4}''$ holes edgewise through four of the 28'' pieces $1\frac{1}{8}''$ from one end. Through two more 28'' pieces, drill these holes at both ends (see drawing 32-1). Sand all wooden parts and apply two coats of polyurethane finish.

Round the corners of the acrylic plastic panels to a 2'' radius, using a coping saw and file. Sand the edge.

On each acrylic panel, mark with a grease pencil the positions of the 48'' pieces. If your panels have a protective paper covering, you'll need to peel it back far enough to allow marking and attaching the wood pieces directly to the panels. Leave the remaining paper on until you've completed the screen.

For each panel, clamp the 48'' pieces in pairs with the acrylic sheet sandwiched between. At positions shown in drawing 32-1, drill through the top 48'' piece and just through the acrylic sheet, using a $\frac{7}{32}''$ bit (drill slowly when piercing the plastic). Use the #10 by $1\frac{1}{2}''$ pilot bit to complete the hole (again, drill slowly). Screw the pieces together with $1\frac{1}{2}''$ by #10 screws.

Next, fasten the 28'' crosspieces to each of the verticals, using glue and 3d nails. Be sure to position those crosspieces such that the $\frac{1}{4}''$ holes line up so you can push the bolts through easily (see drawing 32-1). Then, link the panels together with the $\frac{1}{4}''$ bolts. Set nails and fill holes. Lightly sand wooden parts where you've filled, wipe clean, and touch up with polyurethane oil-sealer finish.

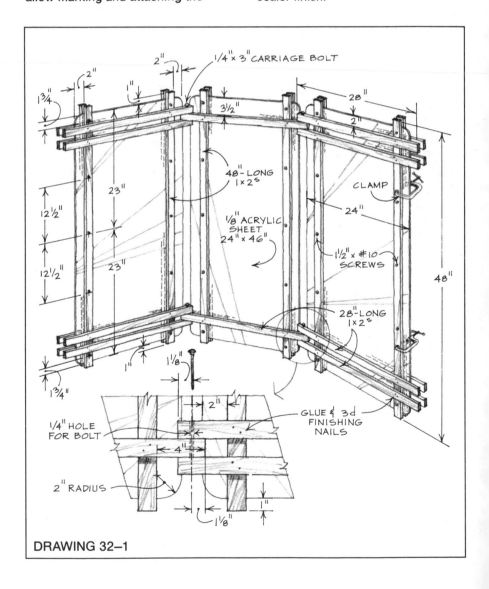

DRAWING 32–1

Clear-top Coffee Table

(Photo on page 30)

Put your coffee cup on this table and it seems to float in space. What holds it there? Transparent acrylic plastic. This type of plastic not only makes a very interesting tabletop, it's also waterproof, easy to work with standard tools, and durable (though it does scratch).

To find a source of acrylic sheet plastic, look in the Yellow Pages under "Plastics." Most dealers will cut the material to size for a minimal fee.

The table's base, like the pieces that accompany it in the photograph on page 30, is made from stock sizes of pine. Joinery is simple—pieces are just glued and nailed together.
Design: Donald Wm. MacDonald

Tools you'll need:

pencil · measuring tape · combination square · crosscut saw or power circular saw · drill with ¼'' bit and a #10 by 1½'' pilot bit · hammer · nailset (or large nail) · screwdriver · sandpaper and finishing tools. *Helpful tools* include a backsaw and miter box, table saw or radial-arm saw, wooden clamps or C-clamps, miter clamps, and power sander.

Materials list

120' of 1 by 2 Clear pine: 20 @ 6'
4' of 2 by 2 Clear pine
10 rust-resistant flathead screws, 1½'' by #10
1 pound of 4d (1½'') galvanized finishing nails
Wood filler (pine)
Waterproof resorcinol glue
1 sheet of acrylic plastic, ¼'' by 30'' by 66''
Strip of foam rubber or felt, ⅛'' by 1½'' by 6''
Polyurethane penetrating oil-sealer finish

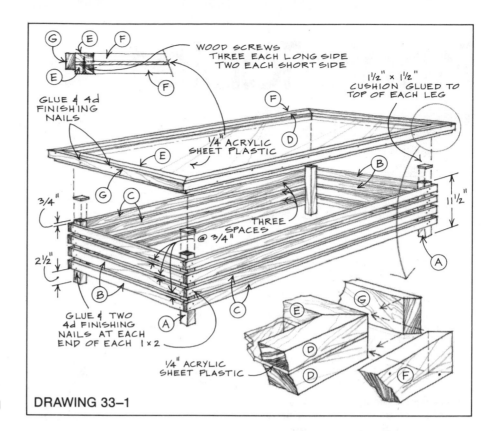

DRAWING 33–1

Here's How

Begin by cutting the pine pieces to size, according to the following cutting list (refer to drawing 33-1). Be sure to use a square for marking and checking your cuts.

(A) Four 2 by 2s, 11½''
(B) Eight 1 by 2s, 27''
(C) Eight 1 by 2s, 64½''
(D) Four 1 by 2s, 66''
(E) Four 1 by 2s, 30''
(F) Two 1 by 2s, 67½''
(G) Two 1 by 2s, 31½''

Assemble the base, as shown in drawing 33-1, using glue and two 4d nails at each end of each 1 by 2. First attach (B) to the legs (A), ends flush with the legs' outside edges. Then join the two sets of legs by attaching the (C) pieces. Cut four 1½'' squares from the foam rubber or felt and glue them to the tops of the legs.

While the freshly glued base dries, make the top. Miter at 45° the ends of pieces (D) through (G), as shown in drawing 33-1. Make two separate rectangular frames from the (D) and (E) pieces, gluing and nailing the corners with 4d finishing nails. Miter clamps are handy for aligning and holding the pieces while you nail.

Most acrylic plastic sheet comes with a protective paper backing. If yours has this, peel back about 3'' of it from each side around the plastic sheet's perimeter. Leave the rest on until you've finished the project.

Sandwich the acrylic plastic between the two frames, aligning it flush around the perimeter. You can use wooden clamps or C-clamps to hold the frames in alignment while you're drilling and driving screws—but don't clamp the pieces too tightly or you may crack the plastic.

Choose one side of the plastic for the top surface, then flip it upside down. Using a drill and ¼'' bit, drill holes for screws through the frame, just penetrating the acrylic sheet, as detailed in drawing 33-1. Finish drilling these holes with the pilot bit, countersinking them so screw heads will sit flush with the wood's surface. Drive in the screws. Attach the (F) and (G) pieces to the outside of the frame with glue and 4d finishing nails.

Set all nails and fill the holes. Sand all wooden parts and wipe clean. Apply three coats of polyurethane penetrating oil-sealer to the wood *only* (immediately wipe up any that spills onto the plastic). When the finish dries, remove the protective paper backing from the acrylic plastic sheet.

Picnic Tables

One a classic, one a novel design

Table and Benches

This redwood picnic table set is almost as much a part of Americana as baseball and apple pie. From Maine to California, it weathers the elements in campgrounds, parks, and backyards. Why does it have such enduring popularity? Because it is sturdy, practical, durable, and simple to build.

Tools you'll need:

pencil · measuring tape · combination square · crosscut saw or power circular saw · chisel · rasp · drill with $\frac{5}{32}''$, $\frac{1}{4}''$, $\frac{5}{16}''$, $\frac{3}{4}''$, and $\frac{7}{8}''$ bits and a #10 by $1\frac{3}{4}''$ pilot bit · socket wrench with $\frac{7}{16}''$ and $\frac{1}{2}''$ sockets · sandpaper and finishing tools. *Helpful tools* include a T-bevel, backsaw and miter box, table saw or radial-arm saw, dado blade, and power sander.

Materials list

All hardware and fastenings should be rust-resistant.
46' of 2 by 6 Clear redwood:
  4 @ 10', 1 @ 6'
30' of 2 by 4 Clear redwood:
  3 @ 10'
4' of 2 by 3 redwood
14' of 1 by 4 redwood:
  1 @ 8', 1 @ 6'
6 carriage bolts, $\frac{5}{16}''$ by $4\frac{1}{2}''$, with washers and nuts
14 lag screws, $\frac{1}{4}''$ by $3\frac{1}{2}''$, with washers
4 lag screws, $\frac{1}{4}''$ by 3'', with washers
70 flathead screws, $1\frac{3}{4}''$ by #10

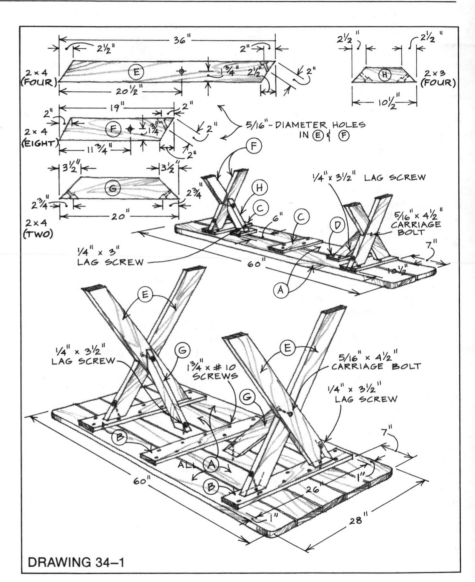

DRAWING 34—1

Waterproof resorcinol glue
Polyurethane penetrating oil-sealer finish

Here's How

Begin by cutting pieces (A) through (D), according to the following cutting schedule. Use a square for marking and checking all cuts.

(A) Nine 2 by 6s, 60''
(B) Three 1 by 4s, 26''
(C) Six 1 by 4s, $10\frac{1}{2}''$
(D) Four 1 by 4s, 6''

Proceed by cutting out the pieces (E) through (H), according to drawing 34-1.

Picnic table and bench set is a sturdy, durable classic.

Lay the top pieces (A) best side down on a clean, flat surface, in groups of two for the benches and five for the table. Space them side by side, $\frac{1}{8}''$ apart (8d box nails work well as spacers), keeping all ends flush with each other.

Set the cleats (B) across the table top pieces, and cleats (C) and (D) across the bench top pieces, positioned as shown in drawing 34-1. Drill countersunk pilot holes for $1\frac{3}{4}''$ by #10 screws where indicated. Remove the (B), (C), and (D) pieces, remembering where they go, spread glue along their undersides, and screw them in place.

Now you can cut the $\frac{3}{4}''$-deep grooves for the interlocking joints in the legs where they cross. To locate these, first drill $\frac{5}{16}''$ holes through the legs where indicated in drawing 34-1. Join pairs of legs by pushing carriage bolts through them. Spread them into an X shape until the distance between their bottom outside corners measures $26\frac{1}{2}''$ for table legs and $15\frac{1}{2}''$ for bench legs. Mark along their edges where they intersect.

Remove carriage bolts and cut slots between the marks, $\frac{3}{4}''$ deep. Unless you have a dado blade, the easiest way to cut these is to make a series of parallel cuts $\frac{3}{4}''$ deep between the marks, then chisel out the waste wood. For more about cutting grooves, see page 68.

Now counterbore and drill pilot holes for the lag screws, as specified in drawing 34-1. Assemble table legs (E) to their braces (G) by pushing $4\frac{1}{2}''$ carriage bolts through the $\frac{5}{16}''$ holes in the legs and in the braces, adding washers, and tightening on nuts. Assemble the bench legs (F) to their braces (H), using the same methods.

Now fasten the table top to the leg assemblies. Work with the top upside down. Set the leg assemblies upside down on the cleats (B). Drill with a $\frac{5}{32}''$ bit through the $\frac{1}{4}''$ holes into the cleats for $\frac{1}{4}''$ by $3\frac{1}{2}''$ lag screws. Put washers on the lag screws and drive them in. Follow the same procedures for the bench legs, except use $3''$ lag screws instead of $3\frac{1}{2}''$ to fasten braces (H) to the cleats labeled (D).

Turn the table and benches right side up on a flat surface. If any of the legs tend to "rock," trim them slightly. Sand all corners, edges, and surfaces until smooth. Apply two or three coats of polyurethane penetrating oil-sealer.

In the table position, swivel-top table offers comfortable seating for dining or games.

Swivel-top Table/Benches

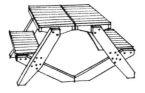

First it's a sturdy picnic table with attached benches on either side, then . . . voilà! It turns into two separate benches with comfortable backrests. What first appears to be a solid table is actually two benches, each having a back that swivels up into horizontal position.
   Design: Ells Marugg

Tools you'll need:

pencil · measuring tape · square · crosscut saw or power circular saw · chisel · drill with $\frac{5}{32}''$, $\frac{1}{4}''$, and $\frac{5}{16}''$ bits and a #8 by $1\frac{1}{2}''$ pilot bit · rasp · hammer · nailset (or large nail) · screwdriver · C-clamps · $\frac{7}{16}''$ and $\frac{1}{2}''$ wrenches · sandpaper and finishing tools. *Helpful tools* include a table saw or radial-arm saw, dado blade, router, socket wrench with $\frac{7}{16}''$ and $\frac{1}{2}''$ sockets, and power sander.

Materials list

All hardware and fastenings should be rust-resistant. Lumber should be Clear redwood or equivalent.
12' of 2 by 6: 2 @ 6'
12' of 2 by 4: 2 @ 6'
22' of 2 by 3: 2 @ 8', 1 @ 6'
16' of 2 by 2: 2 @ 8'
6' of 1 by 6
74' of 1 by 4: 1 @ 14', 5 @ 12'
16 lag screws, $\frac{1}{4}''$ by 2'', with washers
8 carriage bolts, $\frac{5}{16}''$ by 3'', with washers and nuts
16 carriage bolts, $\frac{1}{4}''$ by $3\frac{1}{2}''$, with washers and nuts
20 carriage bolts, $\frac{1}{4}''$ by $2\frac{1}{2}''$, with washers and nuts
8 flathead screws, $1\frac{1}{2}''$ by #8
1 pound of 4d ($1\frac{1}{2}''$) finishing nails
Waterproof resorcinol glue
Wood filler (redwood)
Polyurethane penetrating oil-sealer finish

Here's How

Begin by cutting the pieces to length, according to the following cutting list. Be sure to use a square for marking and checking all cuts.
   Cut all (F) from the the 8-foot 2 by 3s, and cut all (G) from the 6-footer. From each of four 12-foot 1 by 4s, cut six (E) and two (H); from the

remaining 12-footer, cut two (E) and seven (H); from the 14-footer, cut eleven (H).

(A) Four 2 by 6s, $34\frac{1}{4}''$
(B) Four 2 by 4s, 33''
(C) Four 1 by 6s, $16\frac{1}{2}''$
(D) Four 2 by 2s, $47\frac{13}{16}''$
(E) Twenty-six 1 by 4s, 18''
(F) Four 2 by 3s, $47\frac{7}{8}''$
(G) Four 2 by 3s, $12\frac{1}{2}''$
(H) Twenty-six 1 by 4s, 14''

   Cut the (A) and (B) pieces to shape, according to drawing 37-1. Pair them up into four sets—two right-side sets and two left-side sets. When drilling holes and cutting the interlocking joints in these pieces, you must remember that two pairs are mirror images of the other two pairs—the 2 by 6 piece goes on the outside of each frame.
   Mark the holes shown in drawing 37-1 on one side of half the (A) and (B) pieces and on the opposite side of the remaining ones. On the same sides of the (A) and (B) pieces as the hole marks, draw the dotted lines that show the approximate points of overlap.
   Drill the holes in (A) and (B) that are specified in drawing 37-1. Be sure to drill straight (see page 70).
   As shown in drawing 37-2, cross

Swivel-top table—suddenly it's benches.

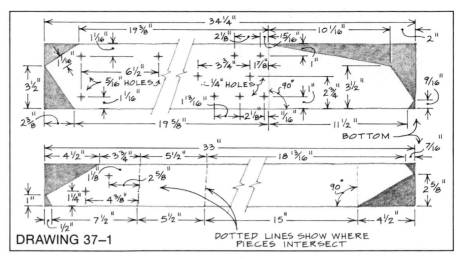

an (A) piece over its mating (B) piece. Edges of the companion pieces should line up with the overlap marks. Adjust them so that the distance between the outer lower edges of the legs is 29¼″ (refer to drawing 37-2). Clamp the pieces together and recheck the measurement. Stand the assembly up on a level surface to make sure the legs sit flat when upright. Mark along the edges of the (A) and (B) pieces exactly where they overlap.

Unclamp the pieces and cut the ¾″-deep interlocking grooves. To cut these, you can either make several cuts with a saw, then chisel out the waste wood; make several passes with a dado blade; or use a router.

Fit the pieces together and clamp again. Drill ¼″ holes through both pieces where marked. Unclamp, spread glue in the grooves, and bolt together with ¼″ by 2½″ carriage bolts—push through from the (A) side and put washers under the nuts. Also drill the remaining holes in (A).

Repeat these steps for the other three side frames, remembering that two of the frames are mirror images of the other two.

Assemble the seat and table top pieces as shown in drawing 37-2. Notice that you must first cut (C) to shape and rabbet the ends of (D) and (F). Glue, and use the fasteners specified in the drawing. Round the edges of the (E) and (H) pieces, using a rasp or sander.

You'll probably need a helper for fastening the seat and top to the side frames. (Assemble one bench at a time.) First clamp the seat to the sides, positioned as detailed in drawing 37-2. Be sure the seat is reasonably level, then using the ¼″ holes in (A) and (B) as guides, drill

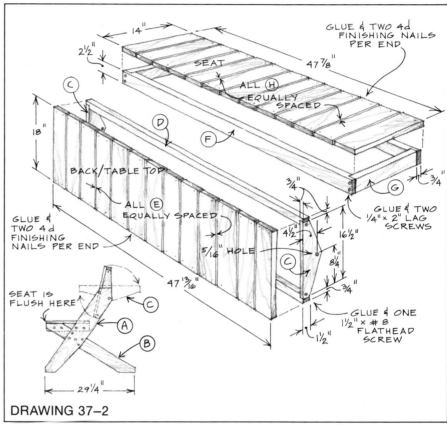

with a ¼″ bit through (G). Push ¼″ by 3½″ carriage bolts through from (A) and (B), add washers, and tighten on nuts. (Don't glue if you want to be able to dismantle the benches.)

Next, drill in (C) the $\frac{5}{16}$″ hole specified in drawing 37-2. Bolt the top in place between the (A) pieces, pushing two $\frac{5}{16}$″ by 3″ carriage bolts through (A) into (C)—one at each end. Check to see that the top pivots freely on those two bolts. If it doesn't, add washers between (C) and (A). Assemble with washers and nuts and tighten.

Now level the top in the table

position and clamp it there. Using the top $\frac{5}{16}$″ hole in (A) as a guide, drill through (C) at both ends. When you want to use the bench as a table, push $\frac{5}{16}$″ by 3″ bolts through these holes.

Tip the top down until the bottom edge is flush with the backside of (A). Clamp the pieces in place and drill through the lower $\frac{5}{16}$″ holes. Put bolts in these holes when you want to use the benches separately.

Set all nails and fill the holes. Sand surfaces, corners, and edges smooth; wipe clean. Apply two or three coats of polyurethane.

Formal Furniture

Modules, chairs, table, and serving cart

Redwood Modules

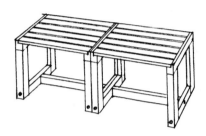

You decide what to do with these handy little redwood modules. Use them individually as stools, footrests, small tables, or plant stands; bunch them for benches or larger tables. If you have a table saw or radial-arm saw, making them is a cinch.

Design: Peter O. Whiteley

Tools you'll need:

pencil · measuring tape · combination square · table saw or radial-arm saw · drill with $\frac{5}{32}''$, $\frac{1}{4}''$, and $\frac{3}{4}''$ bits · hammer · nailset (or large nail) · socket wrench with $\frac{7}{16}''$ socket · sandpaper and finishing tools. *Helpful tools* include a dado blade and power sander.

Materials list (for one module)

12′ of 2 by 3 Clear redwood
10′ of 1 by 3 Clear redwood
10 zinc-plated lag screws, $\frac{1}{4}''$ by 3″, with washers
2 dozen 4d (1$\frac{1}{2}''$) galvanized finishing nails
Waterproof resorcinol glue
Wood filler (redwood)
Polyurethane penetrating oil-sealer finish

Here's How

Begin by cutting the pieces to size, according to the following cutting list. If you're making more than one module, plan to cut all like pieces at the same time. Use a square for marking and checking all cuts. (For more about cutting, see page 67.)

(A) Four 2 by 3s, 14$\frac{5}{8}''$
(B) Two 2 by 3s, 17″
(C) Two 2 by 3s, 12$\frac{1}{4}''$
(D) One 2 by 3, 17″
(E) Six 1 by 3s, 19″

Rip one edge off the (A), (B), and (C) pieces, narrowing them to 2$\frac{3}{8}''$. Then rabbet the opposite edge of (B), 1″ wide and $\frac{3}{4}''$ deep (see drawing 39-1).

Counterbore $\frac{3}{4}''$-diameter, $\frac{3}{4}''$-deep holes in the (A) and (B) pieces, where shown in drawing 39-2.

Modules, table, and chairs are made from stock sizes of redwood.

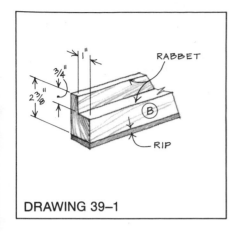

DRAWING 39–1

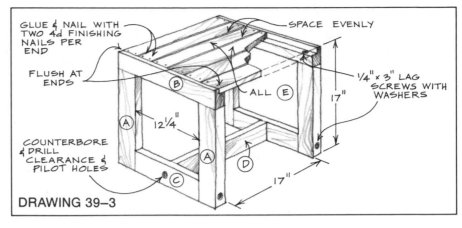

GLUE & NAIL WITH TWO 4d FINISHING NAILS PER END

FLUSH AT ENDS

SPACE EVENLY

¼" x 3" LAG SCREWS WITH WASHERS

17"

12¼"

ALL (E)

COUNTERBORE & DRILL CLEARANCE & PILOT HOLES

17"

DRAWING 39–3

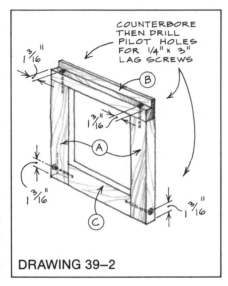

COUNTERBORE THEN DRILL PILOT HOLES FOR ¼" x 3" LAG SCREWS

DRAWING 39–2

Center a ¼" bit in these holes and drill through.

Assemble the two side frames separately, using glue and ¼" by 3" lag screws, as follows: Face the ripped edges of the four pieces inward and butt the pieces together as shown in drawing 39-2. Push a ¼" bit or long nail through holes in (A) and (B) pieces to mark position of the pilot holes on the ends of the (A) and (C) pieces. With the 5/32" bit, drill about an inch into the ends at these locations.

Put a washer onto each lag screw, spread glue on the pieces where they will join, and screw them together, drawing the joints tight with a socket wrench (be careful not to overtighten—you could split the

wood). Let the glue dry.

Now join the two side frames, with rabbeted grooves facing each other (see drawing 39-3). Start by counterboring ¾"-diameter, ½"-deep holes in the (C) pieces, then centering a ¼" bit in these holes and drilling through. Join (D) to the (C) pieces, using the same assembly methods you used for the side frames.

Evenly space the six 1 by 3s (E) in the rabbeted grooves. Glue and nail them in place, using two 4d finishing nails at the end of each (E) piece. Set the nails and fill the holes. Sand the edges and corners smooth and wipe clean. Apply two or three coats of polyurethane penetrating oil-sealer.

Square Dining Table
(Photo on facing page)

Contemporary styling and simple construction make this square redwood table an appealing project for home woodworkers. Not only is it lightweight enough to move easily, it also disassembles quickly into flat sections for winter storage.

For this, as for the other pieces shown at left, you'll need a table saw or radial-arm saw.

Design: Peter O. Whiteley

Tools you'll need:
See list on the facing page. In addition, you'll need a chisel.

Materials list
40' of 2 by 3 Clear redwood:
  1 @ 14', 1 @ 10', 2 @ 8'
48' of 1 by 3 Clear redwood:
  4 @ 10', 1 @ 8'
12 zinc-plated lag screws, ¼" by 3", with washers
½ pound of 4d (1½") galvanized finishing nails
Waterproof resorcinol glue
Wood filler (redwood)
Polyurethane penetrating oil-sealer finish

Here's How

Begin by cutting the various pieces according to drawings 40-1 and 40-2 (next page) and the following cutting list. Be sure to use a square for marking and checking all cuts.

Cut all of (A) from the 10-foot 2 by 3; cut one (B) and one (C) from each of two 8-footers; cut the remaining two (C) and (D) from a 14-footer. Cut three (E) pieces from each of the four 10-foot 1 by 3s; cut two (E) from the 8-footer.

(A) Four 2 by 3s, 28½"
(B) Two 2 by 3s, 50"
(C) Four 2 by 3s, 41"
(D) Two 2 by 3s, 38"
(E) Fourteen 1 by 3s, 39⅞"

Cut 2¼"-wide by 1¼"-deep dadoes in the legs (A), as shown in drawing 40-1. Also counterbore ¾"-diameter by ½"-deep holes and ¼" clearance holes in (A) at positions shown in that drawing.

Rip both edges of each (B), narrowing it to 2¼". At the center of each (B) piece, cut a notch for an interlocking joint (see pages 69 and 74). The width of each notch should be exactly the same as the thickness

(Continued on next page)

. . . Continued from page 39

of the 2 by 3s (about $1\frac{1}{2}''$); its depth should be $1\frac{1}{8}''$. Be sure to cut these notches carefully so they will fit together snugly. Use a chisel to remove waste wood from the cuts.

Now assemble the two base frames, fitting the ends of the crosspieces (B) into the dadoes in the legs (A). Notice that the notch in one crosspiece (B) should face upward, the other downward.

Push a $\frac{1}{4}''$ bit through holes in (A) pieces to mark positions of pilot holes in (B) crosspieces. Take apart, and drill $\frac{5}{32}''$ pilot holes in ends of crosspieces. Spread glue on the pieces where they will join. Lag-screw them together, placing a washer on each lag screw before driving it in with a $\frac{7}{16}''$ socket (don't overtighten). Let the glue dry.

Cut a $\frac{3}{4}''$-deep by $1''$-wide rabbet along one edge of each (C) piece as detailed in drawing 40-2. Also miter the ends at a 45° angle (see the main drawing for directions of miters), and bevel ends of (D) (see detail).

Counterbore $\frac{3}{4}''$-diameter by $\frac{1}{2}''$-deep holes where shown—one hole $\frac{3}{4}''$ from each end of two (C) pieces, and one hole 10″ from each end of the other two (C) pieces. Drill $\frac{1}{4}''$ clearance holes, centered in the counterbored holes.

Join the four (C) pieces in a square with identical pieces opposite each other; be sure all corners are 90°. Push a $\frac{1}{4}''$ bit through the clearance holes nearest the ends, and mark pilot hole locations on mating parts; drill with a $\frac{5}{32}''$ bit.

Spread glue on the mitered ends and lag-screw them together, putting a washer onto each lag screw before driving it in. Also glue and lag-screw the crosspieces (D) in place.

Lay the fourteen 1 by 3s (E) across the frame, evenly spaced. Be sure the two at the ends are snug against the (C) pieces. Glue and nail them in place with two 4d finishing nails at each end of each (E) board and two into each crosspiece (D). Set the nails.

Fill holes and sand all pieces. Wipe clean and apply two coats of polyurethane penetrating oil-sealer. Let dry. Set top on base.

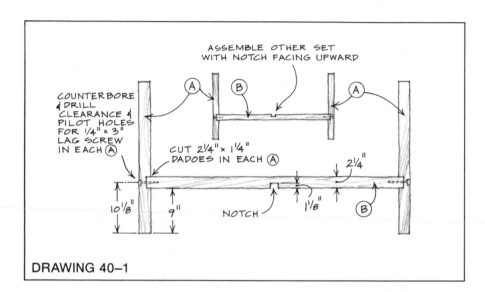

DRAWING 40—1

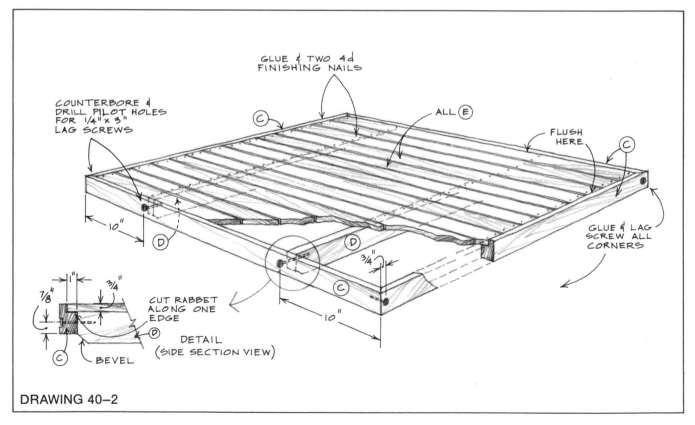

DRAWING 40—2

Dining Chairs

(Photo on page 38)

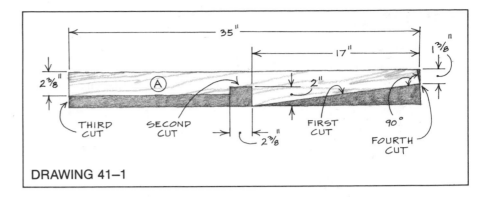

DRAWING 41—1

For those who like to have something to lean back against, here are comfortable, contemporary outdoor chairs. Actually these chairs are just a simple extension of the modules described on page 38. The only real difference is that the back leg is made from a 2 by 4 (instead of a 2 by 3) and extends up to support the chair's back.

Design: Peter O. Whiteley

Tools you'll need:

See list on page 38.

Materials list (for one chair)

6' of 2 by 4 Clear redwood
10' of 2 by 3 Clear redwood
15' of 1 by 3 Clear redwood:
  1 @ 8', 1 @ 7'
10 zinc-plated lag screws, $\frac{1}{4}$" by 3",
  with washers
3 dozen 4d ($1\frac{1}{2}$") galvanized
  finishing nails
Waterproof resorcinol glue
Wood filler (redwood)
Polyurethane penetrating oil-sealer
  finish

Here's How

First cut the pieces to the lengths indicated in the following cutting list. If you're making more than one module, cut all like pieces at the same time. Use a square for marking and checking all cuts.

(A) Two 2 by 4s, 35"
(B) Two 2 by 3s, 17"
(C) Two 2 by 3s, $13\frac{3}{4}$"
(D) Two 2 by 3s, $15\frac{5}{8}$"
(E) One 2 by 3, 17"
(F) Nine 1 by 3s, 19"

Next, shape the back legs (A) as illustrated in drawing 41-1—be sure to make the cuts in the order shown.

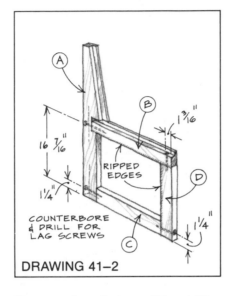

DRAWING 41—2

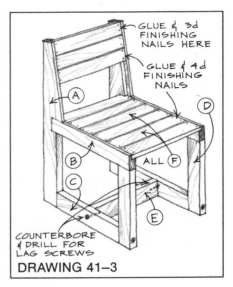

DRAWING 41—3

Rip one edge off pieces (B) and (D), narrowing them to $2\frac{3}{8}$".

Now cut a $\frac{3}{4}$"-deep by 1"-wide rabbet along the edge opposite the ripped edge of each (B) piece, (see drawing 41-2). Cut the same size rabbet along the upper angled part of the back legs (A). *Be sure to treat these as mirror images of each other—cut rabbets on opposite sides of the (A) pieces.*

Assemble the two side frames individually, as follows: Fit (B) into (A), with rabbets facing the same direction and upward. Face the ripped edge of (D) inward (see drawing 41-2). Counterbore $\frac{3}{4}$"-diameter holes $\frac{3}{4}$" deep, and drill $\frac{1}{4}$"-diameter clearance holes, and $\frac{5}{32}$" pilot holes for lag screws in (A), (B), (C), and (D), where shown in drawing 41-2.

Glue and lag-screw together the side frame members (put a washer on each lag screw before driving it in with a socket wrench). Be careful not to overtighten. Let the glue dry.

Next, join the two side frames, (rabbet grooves facing inward) with crosspiece (E), as shown in drawing 41-3. To do this, counterbore $\frac{3}{4}$"

holes $\frac{1}{2}$" deep and drill $\frac{1}{4}$" clearance holes in (C). Drill $\frac{5}{32}$" pilot holes through (C) into (E). Spread glue on the pieces where they will join, and fasten with lag screws through (C) into (E). (Remember to put washers on the lag screws.)

Evenly space the six seat 1 by 3s (F), sliding the back one into the groove in (A). Check for fit, then glue and nail them in position with two 4d finishing nails at each end of each board. Set the nails.

Glue and nail the three back 1 by 3s (F) in place, the top one flush with the top of (A) and the others spaced the same distance apart as the seat 1 by 3s. Use two 4d nails at each end of each board, except for the top board—there, either use 3d finishing nails or bend over and set ends of 4d nails so they don't project. Set nails.

Fill all nail holes and sand all pieces. Wipe clean, then apply two or three coats of polyurethane penetrating oil-sealer.

Serving Cart

(Photo on facing page)

From garden to gazebo, patio to poolside, dining room to deck—this handsome serving cart follows the movements of party guests like an efficient butler. Wherever the party goes, the cart follows, laden with drinks and food.

You can make the whole set shown on page 38 if you wish, or make just the cart—to complement furnishings you already have.

The cart was made from All-Heart redwood; the wheels were purchased from a bicycle shop.

Design: Peter O. Whiteley

Tools you'll need:

pencil · measuring tape · square · table saw or radial-arm saw · coping saw · rasp · hacksaw · drill with $\frac{5}{32}''$, $\frac{1}{4}''$, $\frac{7}{16}''$, and $\frac{3}{4}''$ bits, and #8 by 2'' and #14 by $2\frac{1}{4}''$ pilot bits · hammer · nailset (or large nail) · screwdriver · socket wrench with $\frac{7}{16}''$ socket · sandpaper and finishing tools. *Helpful tools* include a band saw or saber saw, dado blade, and power sander.

Materials list

All hardware and fastenings should be rust-resistant.
20' of 2 by 3 Clear redwood:
  1 @ 12', 1 @ 8'
42' of 1 by 3 Clear redwood:
  3 @ 12', 1 @ 6'
4 lag screws, $\frac{1}{4}''$ by 3''
4 lag screws, $\frac{1}{4}''$ by $3\frac{1}{2}''$
4 flathead screws, 2'' by #8
4 flathead screws, $2\frac{3}{4}''$ by #14
4 flathead screws, $2\frac{1}{4}''$ by #14
$\frac{1}{2}$ pound of 4d ($1\frac{1}{2}''$) finishing nails
2 rubber-tired wheels, 12'' diameter
2 hub nuts, $\frac{7}{16}''$ diameter
6 washers, $\frac{7}{16}''$
30'' steel rod, $\frac{7}{16}''$
Waterproof resorcinol glue
Wood filler (redwood)
Polyurethane penetrating oil-sealer finish

Here's How

Begin by cutting the various pieces to size, according to the following cutting list (refer to drawing 42-1). Be sure to use a square for making and checking your cuts. For more about cutting, refer to page 67.

Cut all of (A) and (B) from the 12' length of 2 by 3. From the 8-footer, cut all of (C), (D), and (E). Cut seven of (F) from each of two 12-foot 1 by 3s; cut four of (F), two of (G), and one of (H) from the third 12-footer; and cut three of (H) from the 6-footer.

(A) Four 2 by 3s, 20''
(B) Two 2 by 3s, $29\frac{1}{2}''$
(C) Two 2 by 3s, $24\frac{3}{4}''$
(D) Two 2 by 3s, 9''
(E) Two 2 by 3s, $6\frac{3}{4}''$
(F) Eighteen 1 by 3s, 20''
(G) Two 1 by 3s, 19''
(H) Four 1 by 3s, 21''

On the table saw or radial-arm saw, rip one edge off of the (A) and (B) pieces, narrowing them to exactly $2\frac{3}{8}''$. At the opposite edge of (B) and along one edge of (C), rabbet a 1'' by 1'' groove, as detailed in drawing 42-1 (detail A).

Next measure the thickness of the 1 by 3 stock. It should be about $\frac{3}{4}''$.

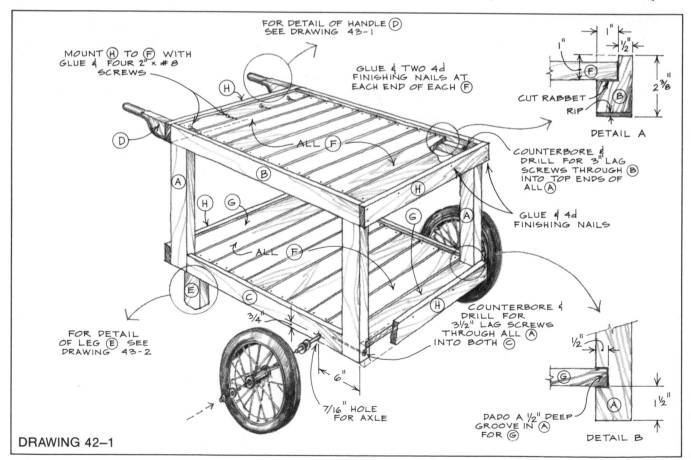

DRAWING 42-1

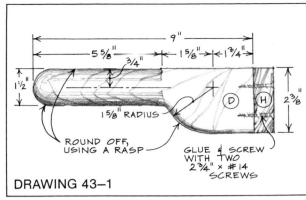

DRAWING 43—1

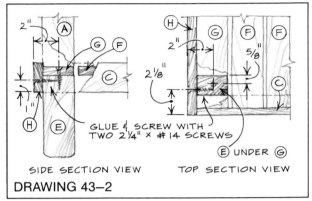

SIDE SECTION VIEW   TOP SECTION VIEW

DRAWING 43—2

Serving cart trails garden party guests.

As shown in drawing 42-1 (detail B), dado a $\frac{1}{2}$''-deep groove in (A), located $1\frac{1}{2}$'' up from one end, that matches that thickness of (G) (about $\frac{3}{4}$'').

Now you're ready to fasten the legs (A) to the horizontal framing members (B) and (C) to make up the two side frame assemblies (refer to drawing 42-1). Counterbore $\frac{3}{4}$''-diameter holes $\frac{3}{8}$'' deep in (A) and (B) where shown, for recessing the lag screws. Center a $\frac{1}{4}$'' bit in those holes and drill clearance holes through (B) into (A) and through (A) into (C). Finish drilling pilot holes in ends of (A) and (C) with a $\frac{5}{32}$'' bit. Glue and screw the pieces together, slipping a washer onto each lag screw.

Let the glue dry, then sand the frames. Stand them up and fit the (G) pieces into the dadoes you cut in the legs (A). Space the (F) pieces evenly, about $\frac{1}{2}$'' apart, along the rabbeted edges of (B) and (C). Glue and nail them in place, then set the nails. Use two 4d finishing nails at each end of each board (see drawing 42-1).

Trim the 1 by 3 (H) pieces to match the width of the 2 by 3s (B) and (C).

Cut out the handles, according to drawing 43-1. Use a coping saw, band saw, or saber saw for cutting them to rough shape, and a rasp for forming them; then sand. Glue and screw one of them flush to each end of one of the (H) boards, first drilling pilot holes for countersinking the $2\frac{3}{4}$'' by #14 screws (see drawing 43-1 for details).

Mount this (H) piece at one upper end of the cart, screwing and gluing it into the edge of the end (F) board. (Be sure to drill pilot holes for countersinking the 2'' by #8 screws.)

Glue and nail the three remaining (H) pieces in place, using 4d finishing nails.

Now sand all of the wooden parts of the cart and fill nail holes and screw holes with wood filler. Sand again and seal with one coat of polyurethane penetrating oil-sealer finish.

Here's how to mount the wheels: Drill $\frac{7}{16}$'' holes for the axle, placed where shown in drawing 42-1. Put a

hub nut on one end of the axle, then one washer, then a wheel, then two more washers. Push the axle through both holes in the cart and hold it snugly in place. Mark the axle where it exits from the cart (at C). Measure the distance on the other side—where the wheel is—from (C) out to the end of the hub nut. From the mark you've made on the axle, measure that distance plus $\frac{1}{8}$'' (for clearance) and cut off the axle at that point, using a hacksaw. (You'll probably want to remove the axle to do the cutting.) Push the axle back through the holes and reverse the assembly sequence to attach the other wheel.

Now measure the distance from the bottom of (C) to the ground with the cart level, and add $1\frac{1}{2}$'' (this should be $6\frac{3}{4}$''). Round the corners at one end of (E). Drill pilot holes for $2\frac{1}{4}$'' by #14 screws, where shown in detail drawing 43-2. Screw through (G) from the top and through (H) from the end.

Add one more coat of polyurethane oil-sealer to all wooden parts of the cart.

Picnic Box/Table

Converts for on-the-run fun

Picnic Box/Table

Here's a wooden picnic "basket" that does it all! It packs plates, cups, placemats, food—you name it. Then when you arrive at your destination, you can unfold it, unpack it, and turn it over, and it's a table for four (the sides swing up to form the tabletop).

If you have a table saw or radial-arm saw for the cutting, construction is fairly easy.
Design: Christin Pon

Tools you'll need:
pencil · measuring tape · square · hacksaw · coping saw · table saw or radial-arm saw · file · hammer · nailset (or large nail) · screwdriver · sandpaper and finishing tools · sewing equipment and a sewing machine with a heavy-duty needle. *Helpful tools* include a compass, saber saw, and dado blade.

Materials list
All hardware and fastenings should be rust-resistant.
$\frac{1}{2}$ sheet of $\frac{1}{2}''$ lumber-core A-B birch plywood, 4' by 4'
3' of hardwood doweling, $\frac{1}{2}''$
2' of chamfer strip
4 dozen 4d ($1\frac{1}{2}''$) finishing nails
2 pairs of fixed-pin hinges, $1\frac{1}{2}''$
2 continuous hinges, $1\frac{1}{16}''$ by 30'', with screws
2 wooden curtain rings, $1\frac{3}{4}''$ i.d.
3 yards of cotton webbing, 2''
$\frac{3}{4}$ yard of 60''-wide army duck (#8)
Matching cotton-wrapped polyester thread
11'' of hook-and-pile closure, 2''
Wood filler (birch)
Waterproof plastic-resin glue
Clear polyurethane exterior finish

Here's How

First cut out all the plywood pieces, as shown in drawing 44-1. As detailed in drawing 45-1, also mark and cut the rabbets and dadoes in the (B), (C), and (D) pieces; cut the handle holes in (D); and cut the gate legs from the (E) pieces.

As shown in drawing 45-2, assemble the (B), (C), and (D) pieces with glue and nails. Cut four pieces of the chamfer strip to 6'' length and glue and nail them in the four inside corners. Make sure all corners are square.

With a hacksaw, cut the continuous hinges to 27''. Smooth cut edges with a file, and screw the hinges in place along the edges of

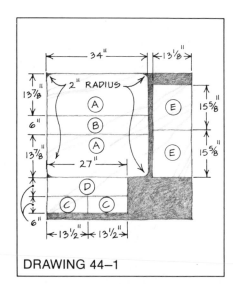

DRAWING 44–1

Picnic box unfolds to become a table.

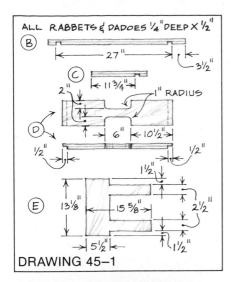

ALL RABBETS & DADOES ¼" DEEP X ½"

DRAWING 45—1

Folded up, it holds picnic makings.

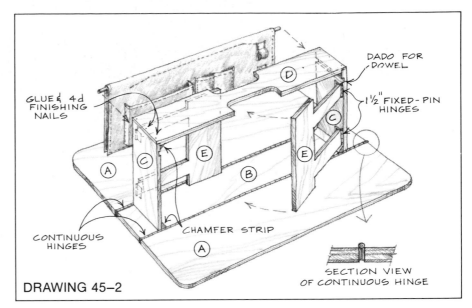

GLUE & 4d FINISHING NAILS

CONTINUOUS HINGES

CHAMFER STRIP

DADO FOR DOWEL

1½" FIXED-PIN HINGES

SECTION VIEW OF CONTINUOUS HINGE

DRAWING 45—2

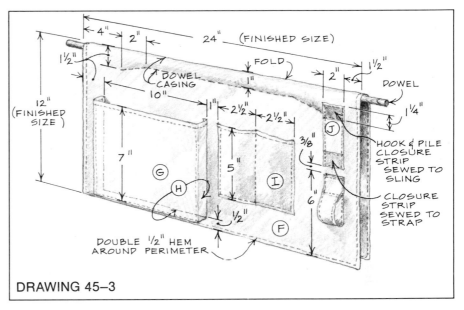

24" (FINISHED SIZE)

DOWEL CASING

FOLD

DOWEL

12" (FINISHED SIZE)

DOUBLE ½" HEM AROUND PERIMETER

HOOK & PILE CLOSURE STRIP SEWED TO SLING

CLOSURE STRIP SEWED TO STRAP

DRAWING 45—3

the (A) and (B) pieces. Mount the legs (E) with hinges to the (C) pieces. Be sure the bottom of the legs align with the outside surface of (D) so they clear the hinge.

Set nails and fill holes. Sand surfaces and edges smooth. Apply two coats of polyurethane finish.

Before you make the pouch and straps, cut the dowel to fit in the dadoes on the inside of (C)—approximately $26\frac{7}{16}''$.

To make the cloth sling, begin by cutting out the pieces. You need one main body (F) at 26" by 26"; two plate pockets (G) at $8\frac{1}{4}''$ by $10\frac{1}{2}''$; two plate pocket bands (H) at $1\frac{3}{4}''$ by 26"; two utensil pockets (I) at $5\frac{1}{2}''$ by $6\frac{1}{4}''$; and four cup straps (J) at 3" by $4\frac{1}{2}''$.

Sew a double ½" hem along all four sides of the main body (F). Mark positions of pockets, straps, and closure strips on the main body, according to drawing 45-3. (Only one side of the sling is pictured; reverse positions on the flip side.)

Along one long edge of the plate

pocket band (H), fold under and press ¼". Pin the unfolded edge of the band along sides and bottom of pocket (G) with right sides together and join with a ¼" seam. Make a double ½" hem on pocket's top edge. Topstitch pocket to main body along folded edge of band.

On utensil pocket, make a double ½" hem at the top, then fold under ¼" on remaining edges. Topstitch to sling. Divide pocket in half with a vertical seam.

For each cup strap (J), make a double ¼" hem on the long sides. On one end turn under ¼", then sew a closure strip ($1\frac{1}{4}''$ long) on the wrong side of the strap, enclosing the raw edge. Position the strap on the main body (F) with *right* sides

together, then sew the matching closure strip to (F), covering ¼" of the other raw edge of the strap.

Fold sling in half (as in photo), then sew a casing near the fold to hold the dowel.

Cut two 54" lengths of webbing and sew a double $\frac{3}{8}''$ hem in one end of each. Starting $1\frac{1}{4}''$ from that end, sew a 3"-long closure strip to the right side of the same strap; sew its mate 13" from the end. Thread other end through a wooden ring, fold over $\frac{3}{8}''$, and sew to wrong side of strap $3\frac{1}{2}''$ from ring.

To secure closed picnic box, wrap the straps around box, thread loose ends of straps through wooden rings, and press closure strips together.

Gazebo is an oasis for eating, drinking, conversation. This photo shows it with top in place.

Without top, gazebo offers sunny seating.

Garden Gazebo

Entertains in summer, stores away in winter

Garden Gazebo

(Photos on facing page)

For poolside parties, garden gatherings, or informal interaction, this gazebo is ideal! It's a focal point—a center for festivities or a place to sit and chat or enjoy a relaxed meal.

It is designed to be very easy to build: Key elements automatically become patterns for all other elements, so you don't have to calculate any angles. It's made from standard lumber and plywood. And, because the main parts are bolted together, all you have to do to take it apart and move it or store it flat is twist off a few wing nuts!

And the structure is versatile. You can leave all of the seats in place, or remove a few so it's accessible from several sides. You can suspend a flat basket as a table in the center, or you can hang plants from the rafters. Use it however you wish!

Though the instructions for making the canvas are given last, be sure to plan ahead. If you don't intend to do the sewing yourself, get a professional upholsterer or awning maker started as early as possible, so the top will be finished about the same time as the structure.

Design: William Louis Kapranos

Tools you'll need:

pencil · measuring tape · square · chalk line · crosscut saw or power circular saw · saber saw · drill with a $\frac{5}{16}$'' bit and a #12 by 2½'' pilot bit · hammer · caulking gun · screwdriver · sandpaper and finishing tools. For making the top, you'll also need grommet setting tools, sewing equipment, and a heavy-duty sewing machine. *Helpful tools* include a table saw or radial-arm saw, power sander, and C-clamps.

Materials list

All hardware and fastenings should be rust-resistant.
56' of 2 by 6 construction fir (or grade to suit): 7 @ 8'
60' of 2 by 3 construction fir (or grade to suit): 6 @ 10'
3 sheets of ½'' A-C exterior plywood, 4' by 8'
2 sheets of ½'' C-D exterior plywood, 4' by 8'
1 sheet of ¾'' A-C exterior plywood, 4' by 8'
4 cartridges of waterproof paneling adhesive
1 pound of ⅞'' roofing nails
2 pounds of 6d (2'') box nails
1 pound of 8d (2½'') box nails
1 pound of 16d (3½'') box nails
14 carriage bolts, ¼'' by 3'', with washers and wing nuts
14 carriage bolts, ¼'' by 3½'', with washers and wing nuts
46 flathead screws, 2½'' by #12
3 yards of 36''-wide fade- and shrink-resistant synthetic awning canvas
Matching thread
8 large grommets
8 swivel-locking snap fasteners
Exterior enamel paints

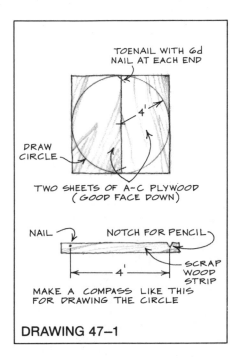

TOENAIL WITH 6d NAIL AT EACH END

4'

DRAW CIRCLE

TWO SHEETS OF A-C PLYWOOD (GOOD FACE DOWN)

NAIL

NOTCH FOR PENCIL

SCRAP WOOD STRIP

4'

MAKE A COMPASS LIKE THIS FOR DRAWING THE CIRCLE

DRAWING 47–1

Here's How

Begin by constructing the floor. Lay two sheets of ½'' A-C exterior plywood, best face down, on a flat, clean surface, forming an 8' square (as shown in drawing 47-1). So they won't separate as you work on them, toenail them together through their edges with one 6d nail at each end.

Locate the center of the 8' square and from this center point, draw a circle with a 4' radius. To make a large compass, notch a wood strip to hold a pencil, then use a nail inserted 4' from the pencil to tack the strip to the center of the square (see drawing 47-1).

With a caulking gun, spread two cartridges of adhesive within the circle. Keep the adhesive about an inch inside the pencil line so it won't squish beyond the line when sandwiched between the panels.

Now lay two ½'' sheets of C-D exterior plywood, good face up, on

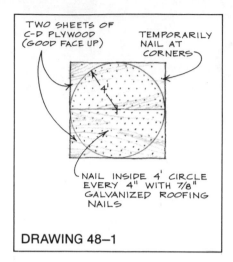

DRAWING 48-1

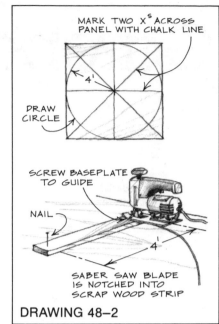

DRAWING 48-2

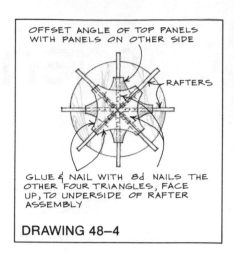

DRAWING 48-4

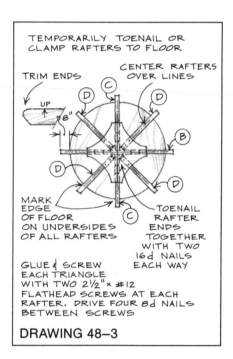

DRAWING 48-3

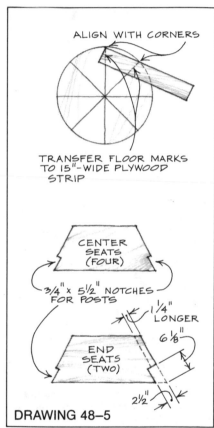

DRAWING 48-5

top of the first two panels but perpendicular to them (see drawing 48-1). Temporarily nail these in place to keep them from moving, then mark a 4'-radius circle on them. Within the circle, nail with $\frac{7}{8}''$ roofing nails spaced 4'' apart. Keep the nails at least an inch inside the pencil line. Remove the temporary nails.

Now turn this 1''-thick, 8' square of plywood over and lay it across a couple of lengths of scrap wood. With a chalk line, mark two large Xs across the panel, as shown in drawing 48-2. Also draw a 4'-radius circle.

Cutting out the circle with a saber saw is next. You can either do this freehand or make a guide like the one detailed in drawing 48-2. If you make the guide, screw the saber saw's baseplate to it for best results. After cutting, set the triangular corner pieces aside for later use and sand the edge around the perimeter of the circle.

Next cut the 2 by 3s and 2 by 6s to length. Be sure to use a square for marking and checking all cuts. Here's what you'll need:

(A) Seven 2 by 6s, $93\frac{1}{2}''$ (posts)
(B) One 2 by 3, 112'' (rafter)
(C) Two 2 by 3s, $55\frac{1}{4}''$ (rafters)
(D) Four 2 by 3s, 53'' (rafters)
(E) Seven 2 by 3s, $12\frac{3}{4}''$ (fillers)
(F) Seven 2 by 3s, $15\frac{1}{4}''$ (floor cleats)

For much of the remaining layout work, you can use the lines chalked on the gazebo floor as guides. They will make your work much easier.

Lay the rafters (B, C, and D) on the floor, centered over the lines, as shown in drawing 48-3. Trim their ends as shown. It's a good idea to toenail the rafters together with 16d nails. Then cut 6'' off of the pointed corners of the $\frac{1}{2}''$ plywood pieces that you set aside earlier. Glue, nail, and screw four of the triangles on top of the rafters, with right angles meeting in the center (see drawing 48-3).

On the underside of each rafter, mark the edge of the circular floor. These marks will come in handy later for getting the posts vertical.

Remove temporary nails and turn over the rafter assembly. Glue, nail, and screw the other four triangular corner pieces to the rafters, at the offsetting angle, with the best side facing up as you nail (see drawing 48-4).

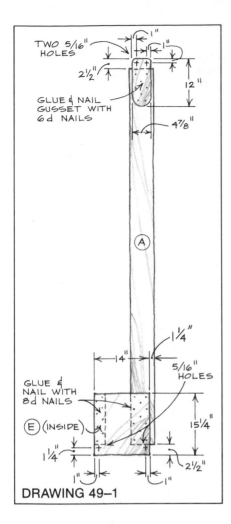

DRAWING 49—1

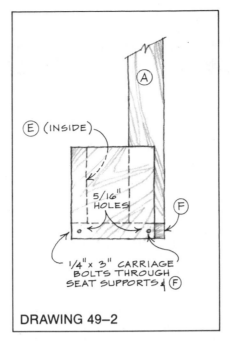

DRAWING 49—2

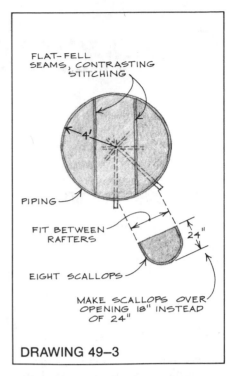

DRAWING 49—3

Next cut a sheet of ¾″ A-C plywood into three 8′ by 15″ strips; these will become the seats. Lay one 15″-wide strip on the floor and transfer the lines of the floor onto it (see drawing 48-5). Cut it off on those lines and notch the corners as shown in the detail. Then use it as a template for marking and cutting three others. For the two end seats, you'll need two additional panels that are 1¾″ longer on one edge; notch these pieces as well.

Now make the gussets for the post tops—you'll need fourteen. Cut them from leftover ¾″ plywood and drill them, following the pattern detailed in drawing 49-1. (Again, you can cut and drill one and use it as a template for the others.)

Glue and nail one gusset to each face at one end of each post, using 6d box nails (six nails per gusset). Be sure the holes of paired gussets match up.

For the seat supports, divide a sheet of ½″ plywood into fourteen pieces, each 14″ by 15¼″. Drill $\frac{5}{16}$″ holes through one piece at the locations detailed in drawing 49-1, and use this as a template for drilling the others. Glue and nail these in pairs in combination with the 2 by 3 fillers (E) to the posts (A) as shown in drawing 49-1.

Center the floor cleats (F) over seven of the chalk lines on the floor (flush with the edge), and glue and nail them there with 16d nails. Turn the floor upside down and screw the floor to each cleat with two 2½″ by #12 wood screws (drill pilot holes with a #12 by 2½″ pilot bit). Turn the floor back over (right side up).

One at a time, set the post assemblies onto the floor cleats (drawing 49-2). Use the holes through the plywood as guides for drilling $\frac{5}{16}$″ holes through the cleats. Push ¼″ by 3″ carriage bolts through, add washers, and tighten on wing nuts.

When all posts are bolted in place, have someone help you lift the roof atop the posts so that the rafters rest between gussets. Use the holes through the gussets as guides for drilling $\frac{5}{16}$″ holes through the rafters. Push ¼″ by 3½″ carriage bolts through, add washers, and tighten on wing nuts.

Here's a tip: it would be wise to label connecting joints in an inconspicuous place so that when you put the gazebo up next time, everything will fit perfectly.

Set the seat tops in place, and sand all wooden pieces—especially the posts and seat tops—until smooth. Before painting, remove the rafter assembly and the seats. Paint the gazebo whatever colors you feel will complement its environment. Let the paint dry, then reassemble.

We had the canvas top made by an awning shop, but you can do the work yourself if you have sewing skills and a heavy-duty sewing machine. For the top, follow the pattern given in drawing 49-3.

To attach the top, screw a swivel-locking fastener 1″ in from the end of each rafter (on the top surface). Grommets in the canvas top align with and receive these fasteners.

Plywood Furniture

This slot-together group stores flat

Triangle Chairs

(Photo on facing page)

Inexpensive, easy to make, and comfortable—these chairs are ideal for informal, outdoor dining. And they knock down into flat sections for easy, minimum-space storage.

What's more, you can make three chairs from one 4' by 8' sheet of plywood (and still have some left over); buy two sheets and make a complete set of six.

Design: Don Vandervort

Tools you'll need:

pencil • measuring tape • compass • square • straightedge • saber saw • crosscut saw or power circular saw • drill with a ¾'' bit • sandpaper and finishing tools. *Helpful tools* include a router with a ⅜''-radius bit, and a ¾'' dado blade for a power saw.

Materials list (for 6 chairs)

2 sheets of ¾'' A-A birch plywood, 4' by 8'
Clear polyurethane exterior finish

Here's How

Mark the cutting lines on the plywood sheet, as shown in drawing 50-1. For exact measurements of the three basic parts, see drawing 50-2. You may find that the easiest way to map out the cutting lines on the plywood is to first lay out and cut one of each part, then use those three parts as templates for marking the other pieces.

Use a crosscut saw or power circular saw for cutting the straight lines; the saber saw works well for curves and corners (start its blade in a ¾'' drilled hole for cutouts). Correct techniques for cutting slots are discussed on page 69. Be sure to cut the slots as accurately as possible. If you cut them too large, the finished chair's joints will be loose; if you cut them too narrow, the pieces won't slide together.

If you have a router equipped with a ⅜''-radius bit, round off all the edges around the perimeter of each piece. This will give the chair a more "finished" look.

Assemble each chair to check pieces for proper fit. Disassemble and make any needed adjustments. Sand the edges lightly and wipe off the dust, then apply two coats of clear polyurethane finish. After the finish dries, reassemble the chairs.

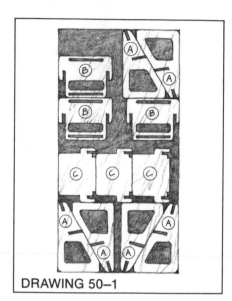

DRAWING 50-1

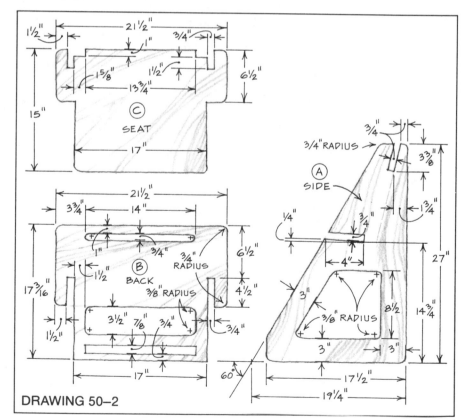

DRAWING 50-2

Triangle chairs and two-level table (in its high position) are comfortable for outdoor dining, knock down when not in use.

Two-level Table

(Photos above and on page 52)

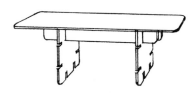

Divide up a sheet of plywood, cut a few slots, and add four barrel bolts. The result: a table that serves up to six people at either dining table or coffee table height and disassembles easily for flat storage when not in use.

Any dining chairs of standard height work well with it when the table is set up as a dining table (although those shown with it are the perfect complement, practically any chairs will do). When the table is at its lower level, guests can sit or kneel on the ground around it.
Design: Don Vandervort

Tools you'll need:

pencil · measuring tape · compass · square · straightedge · coping saw or saber saw · crosscut saw or power circular saw · drill with a $\frac{5}{16}''$ bit · hammer · screwdriver · sandpaper and finishing tools. *Helpful tools* include a router with a $\frac{3}{8}''$-radius bit, and a $\frac{3}{4}''$ dado blade for a power saw.

Materials list

All hardware and fastenings should be rust-resistant.
1 sheet of $\frac{3}{4}''$ A-A birch plywood, 4' by 8'
4 barrel bolts, 2'', with $\frac{3}{4}''$ screws
8 flat strike plates for barrel bolts (optional), with $\frac{3}{4}''$ screws
2 dozen 3d ($1\frac{1}{4}''$) finishing nails
Water-resistant glue
Clear polyurethane exterior finish

Here's How

Begin by marking the cutting lines on the plywood, as shown in drawing 52-1 (next page). Cut out the basic parts, using a crosscut saw or power circular saw. With a compass, mark the corner radii, according to the dimensions in drawing 52-2. Also mark the slots, using a square and a pencil.

Round the corners with a coping saw or saber saw, then sand them to an even roundness. Now cut the slots. Do this work very carefully—the slots must be exactly $\frac{3}{4}''$ wide so they will join snugly. It's better to cut them too narrow and trim them later than to cut them too wide.

Slide the (B) and (C) pieces together to test for a snug fit. Check all four sides of the (C) pieces. Disassemble and make any needed adjustments.

Next, if you have a router with a $\frac{3}{8}''$-radius bit, round off the top edges of the tabletop (A). Sand all edges until smooth.

Turn the tabletop (A) upside down (set it on a couple of scraps of lumber to protect it). Assemble the base (B) and (C) and center it on the underside of (A), as shown in drawing 52-2 (next page). Attach the small blocks (D) to the top (A) with glue and 3d finishing nails.

Position the barrel bolts as shown

in the drawing and determine where the holes for these bolts will go in (C) at both levels. Use a $\frac{5}{16}$″ bit (or one that corresponds to the bolt's diameter) for drilling holes at those locations. If you have purchased strike plates, attach them over the holes. Screw the barrel bolts in place on (D).

Disassemble the table, clean it off, and apply two coats of clear polyurethane exterior finish to the plywood, according to the directions on the label. Let the finish dry, then reassemble.

Two-level Table at its lower level (see page 51)

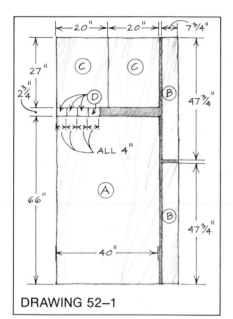

DRAWING 52–1

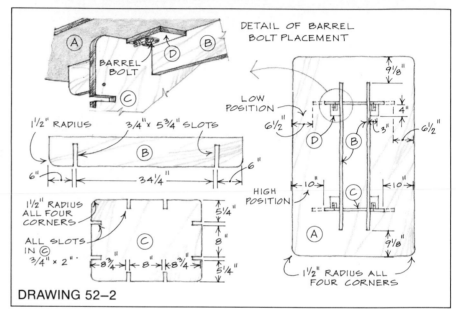

DRAWING 52–2

Knock-down Sun Lounge

(Photos on facing page)

Disassembled, it's just a stack of boards and a lounge cushion, but interlock all of the pieces, and these meager parts become a comfortable, good-looking sun lounge with an adjustable backrest. This project is designed to interlock by simply sliding together its various parts.
Design: Victor Post

Tools you'll need:

pencil · measuring tape · compass · square · straightedge · coping saw or saber saw · crosscut saw or power circular saw · hacksaw · drill with a $\frac{3}{4}$″ bit and a #8 by $1\frac{3}{4}$″ pilot bit · screwdriver · sandpaper and finishing tools. *Helpful tools* include a table saw or radial-arm saw and a $\frac{3}{4}$″ dado blade.

Materials list

All hardware and fastenings should be rust-resistant.
1 sheet of $\frac{3}{4}$″ A-A birch plywood, 4′ by 8′
2′ of continuous hinge, with $\frac{5}{8}$″ screws
5″ of hardwood doweling, $\frac{3}{4}$″
2 flathead screws, $1\frac{3}{4}$″ by #8
Waterproof resorcinol glue
Wood filler (birch)
Clear polyurethane exterior finish

Standard 2′ by 6′ chaise pad (purchase at an outdoor furniture store)

Here's How

First, mark and cut all of the pieces from the plywood sheet, according to drawing 53-1. For more about cutting, see page 67.

Refer to drawing 53-2 for locations of all $\frac{3}{4}$″-wide slots. The easiest way to cut these is to first drill a $\frac{3}{4}$″-diameter hole, then cut into the hole from the edge of the plywood using a crosscut saw or power saw.

Using a compass, mark the various radii for rounding corners, then cut those corners round with a saber saw or coping saw. Sand the corners so that the curves are smooth and even.

Next drill $\frac{3}{4}$″-diameter holes through the pieces labeled (H) and (I) (see drawing 53-2 for location

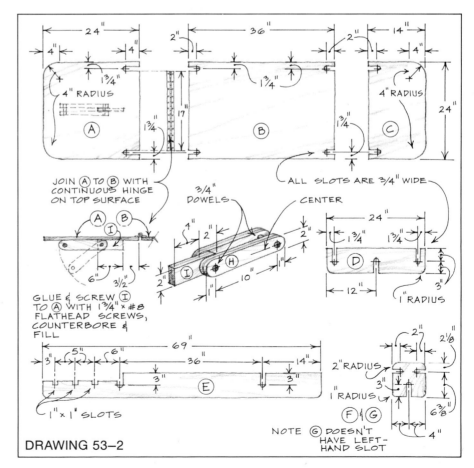

of dowel holes) and cut two 2¼″ lengths of doweling. Sand all pieces. Assemble the entire support, as shown in the drawing, gluing the dowels into the holes of the outside pieces only (the center piece must swing freely).

Attach the support assembly to the underside of piece (A), using glue and the two wood screws, countersinking the screws. Then fill the holes with wood filler.

Sand all pieces, rounding the outside edges slightly. Using a hacksaw, cut the continuous hinge to 19″, then fasten it to (A) and (B) as shown in drawing 53-2. Assemble lounge (refer to photo) and check the pieces for fit; make any necessary adjustments, then slide pieces apart for finishing. Apply two coats of clear polyurethane finish to all wooden pieces (be careful not to let the finish build up in the slots or the parts will be difficult to slide together).

Let the polyurethane dry, slide the pieces back together, lay the lounge pad in place, and you're finished!

Knock-down sun lounge has adjustable backrest for comfortable sunning; stores flat (inset).

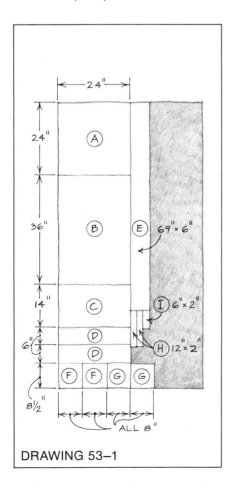

DRAWING 53–1

DRAWING 53–2

Fold-up Furniture Set

Elegantly designed from pine and canvas

Collapsible Pine Table

This beautifully designed pine table is elegant enough to be used indoors, yet sturdy and durable enough for outdoor dining. It seats four comfortably and knocks down quickly into three folding sections.
  Design: Duane Haggerty, Pine Design

Tools you'll need:

pencil • measuring tape • framing square • crosscut saw or power circular saw • drill with $\frac{3}{8}''$ and $\frac{3}{4}''$ and a #8 by $2\frac{1}{2}''$ pilot bit • hammer • screwdriver • needle-nose pliers • socket wrench with a $\frac{1}{2}''$ socket • sandpaper and finishing tools. *Helpful tools* include a table saw or radial-arm saw, drill press, and power sander.

Materials list

All hardware and fastenings should
  be rust-resistant.
14' of 2 by 4 Clear pine
20' of 2 by 3 Clear pine: 2 @ 10'
16' of 2 by 2 pine or fir: 2 @ 8'
116' of 1 by 2 Clear pine: 8 @ 12',
  2 @ 10'
32' of 1 by 1 pine: 4 @ 8'
16 machine bolts, $\frac{5}{16}''$ by 5'', with
  washers and square nuts
6 stove bolts, $\frac{1}{4}''$ by $\frac{3}{4}''$, with nuts
20 flathead screws, $2\frac{1}{2}''$ by #8
12 screw eyes, #112
1 pound of 3d ($1\frac{1}{4}''$) finishing nails
4 strap hinges, 2'', with screws
Waterproof plastic resin glue
Wood filler (pine)
Clear polyurethane exterior finish

Sleek pine furniture combines wood and canvas with functional styling, folds for storage (inset).

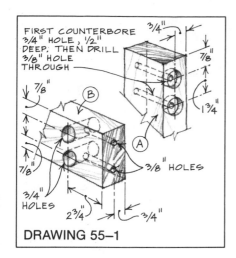

DRAWING 55–1

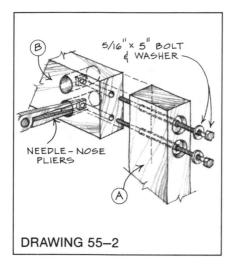

DRAWING 55–2

[Drawing 55–3 — central and right illustrations with labels including: STRAP HINGE, SEE DETAIL A, STRAP HINGE HERE, SCREW EYES & ¾" BOLTS, SCREW EYES & ¾" BOLTS, GLUE & NAIL WITH 3d NAILS, SCREW EYES & ¾" BOLT, DETAIL A, 2½" × #8 SCREWS (PLACE AWAY FROM HINGE LOCATIONS), CUT & HINGE BETWEEN 17TH & 18TH 1×2s, FLUSH WITH SECOND 1×2, ALL H, UNDERSIDE OF TABLE]

DRAWING 55–3

Here's How

Begin by cutting the pieces for the leg-and-rail assembly to size, according to the following cutting list (refer to drawing 55-3). Use a square for marking and checking all cuts. For more about cutting, see page 67.

(A) Eight 2 by 3s, 28½″
(B) Two 2 by 4s, 28″
(C) Two 2 by 4s, 52″
(D) Two 2 by 2s, 56¾″
(E) Two 2 by 2s, 29¾″
(F) Four 1 by 1s, 56¾″
(G) Four 1 by 1s, 29¾″

Set aside two (F) and two (G) pieces for later use. Measure and mark the locations of the ⅜″ and ¾″ holes at the tops of the legs (A), as shown in drawing 55-1.

At each location in (A), counter-bore a ¾″-diameter hole, ½″ deep. Then drill a ⅜″-diameter hole straight through, centered in the larger hole. *Be sure to drill straight* (see page 70).

Hold one leg (A) in place against the end of one rail (B), flush along the top and sides. Drill through the ⅜″ holes into the rail's end, as deep as the ⅜″ drill bit will reach. Then remove the leg (A) and drill the holes in the rail's end at least 2¾″ deep. Repeat for all other leg-to-rail joints. Next, drill the intersecting ¾″-diameter holes in the sides of the rails (B) and (C).

Push a washer onto each 5″ bolt. Spread glue on the ends of the rails and the edges of the legs where they will join. Bolt them together, as shown in drawing 55-2 (with needle-nose pliers, hold a nut inside the ¾″ hole to receive the bolt, which you turn with a socket wrench). Tighten the bolts firmly, then wipe off the excess glue.

Glue and nail one of the (F) 1 by 1s to each (D), and one of the (G) 1 by 1s to each (E), flush at the ends and along one edge, as shown in drawing 55-3. Drill pilot holes for 2½″ by #8 screws—you'll need seven in each (D) 2 by 2 and three in each (E)

2 by 2. Then glue and screw the 2 by 2s to the inner faces of the rails (drawing 55-3).

Join the leg-and-rail assemblies of two corners of the table with strap hinges at the top and screw eyes and ¾″ bolts at the bottom (see drawing 55-3).

Then join the two corner assemblies with four more sets of screw eyes and ¾″ bolts. These are the bolts you'll remove when you want to take apart the frame for storage.

Now use the framing square to make sure your corner joints are at 90° angles. Measure the inside dimensions of the table base—between the two (B) rails and the two (C) rails—to determine the tabletop's exact size. Sizes of (H) and (I) given below are based upon measurements of 33″ and 57″. If your actual measurements differ, make the necessary adjustments. For the top, you'll need:

(H) Thirty-five 1 by 2s, 33″
(I) Two 1 by 2s, 53¼″

(Continued on next page)

. . . Continued from page 55

You'll also need the two (F) and two (G) pieces set aside earlier.

On a flat, clean surface, lay out the thirty-five (H) pieces, good side down. Space them evenly so the overall length is 57''. Use the (I) pieces to keep ends flush, and check with a square to be sure all (H) pieces are perpendicular to (I)

and all corners are square.

Glue and nail (F) in place, flush along the outside edges, using two 3d nails at each end of each 1 by 2 (H) (see drawing 55-3 on page 55). Then glue and nail (G) in place along the end pieces. Also glue and nail the backing 1 by 2s (I) in place.

Cut through the (F) and (I) pieces

at the approximate center of the tabletop, between two top slats, as shown in drawing 55-3. Rejoin the two halves with strap hinges, fastened to (I).

Sand all parts until smooth, rounding corners and edges. Finish with two coats of clear polyurethane finish. Let dry. Set top on base.

Folding Chairs

(Photos on page 54)

Here is a new slant on the outdoor dining chair. These contemporary chairs of pine and canvas are lightweight for easy mobility and comfortable enough to sit on for hours. What's more, they fold flat for minimum-space storage when not in use.

Designed from 1 by 2s, rounds (closet poles), and canvas, they are surprisingly easy to make. For the framework, all you do is cut the pieces to length, drill some holes, and bolt the pieces together.

Design: Duane Haggerty, Pine Design

Tools you'll need:

pencil • measuring tape • square • crosscut saw or power circular saw • file or rasp • drill with $\frac{3}{16}''$, $\frac{3}{8}''$, and $\frac{1}{2}''$ bits • screwdriver • needle-nose pliers • staple gun with staples • sandpaper and finishing tools • sewing machine and sewing equipment. *Helpful tools* include a table saw or radial-arm saw, drill press, and power sander.

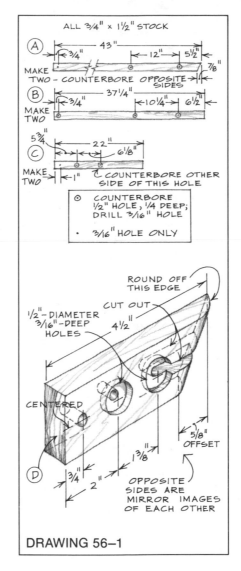

DRAWING 56–1

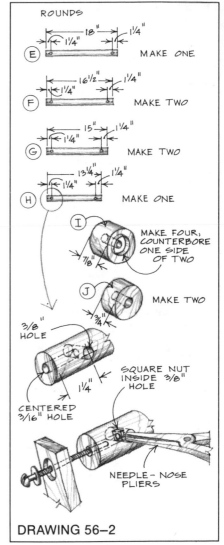

DRAWING 56–2

Materials list (for one chair)

All hardware and fastenings should be rust-resistant.
18' of 1 by 2 Clear pine: 1 @ 8', 1 @ 10'
9' of rounds, $1\frac{5}{16}''$: 1 @ 6', 1 @ 3'
4 stove bolts, $\frac{3}{16}''$ by $3\frac{1}{2}''$
2 stove bolts, $\frac{3}{16}''$ by $2\frac{3}{4}''$
6 stove bolts, $\frac{3}{16}''$ by 2''
2 stove bolts, $\frac{3}{16}''$ by $1\frac{3}{4}''$
2 stove bolts, $\frac{3}{16}''$ by $1\frac{1}{4}''$
14 square nuts, $\frac{3}{16}''$

2 wing nuts, $\frac{3}{16}''$
20 washers, #10
2 fender washers, $\frac{3}{16}''$
$2\frac{1}{4}$ yards of 36''-wide #10 canvas
Matching cotton-wrapped polyester thread
Clear polyurethane exterior finish

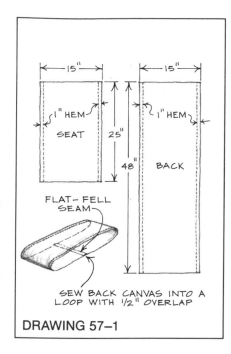

DRAWING 57-1

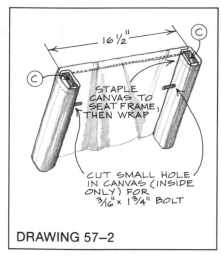

DRAWING 57-2

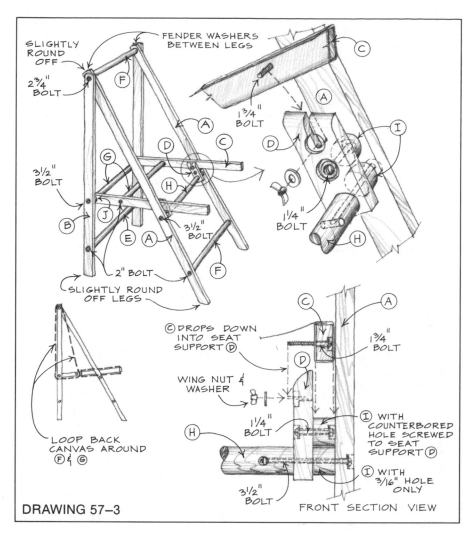

DRAWING 57-3

Here's How

Begin by cutting the 1 by 2s and rounds to length and marking hole placements, as indicated in drawings 56-1 and 56-2 (facing page). Use a square for marking and checking all cuts; measure carefully for bolt holes.

Cut (A) and (D) from the 8'-long 1 by 2; cut (B) and (C) from the 10-footer. From the 6' length of round, cut (E), (F), and (H); cut (G), (I), and (J) from the 3-footer.

At specified locations, counter-bore by drilling $\frac{1}{2}$''-diameter holes approximately $\frac{3}{16}$'' deep. Be sure to drill these holes on the proper sides of the wood pieces (some of the pieces are mirror images of their mates). Then drill $\frac{3}{16}$'' holes through the pieces, centering them in the

counterbored holes. Be sure to drill straight (see page 70).

Slightly round off the ends of the legs, as shown in drawing 57-3, using a file or rasp. Also round off all sharp corners and edges with sandpaper. Sand the surfaces until smooth, then apply two coats of polyurethane exterior finish.

Next make the canvas slings (see drawing 57-1). As you can see, the seat sling is just a rectangle that has its long edges hemmed. The back sling is longer and is sewn in a large loop. For more about making these kinds of slings, see page 76.

Staple the seat sling to the seat frame pieces (C), as shown in drawing 57-2. You should wrap and staple it so that the distance from outer edge to outer edge is exactly 16½''. Add 1¾'' bolts in (C).

Now you're ready to assemble the chair (refer to drawing 57-3). Plan to put a washer under each bolt head and nut, *except* under nuts that are pushed on edge into the

holes in the sides of rounds (see drawing 56-2 for technique of inserting those square nuts).

Join the back legs (B) and the front legs (A) with the top (F) round, first looping the back canvas tube over (F). Add (E) at the bottom of the back legs.

Next connect the seat frame pieces with two (G) rounds, looping the back canvas tube over both rounds and using (J) pieces as spacers between the back (G) round and the back legs (B). (The seat frame should be in the folded-up position to allow enough slack in the back canvas sling for this step.)

When you've finished the assembly, firmly pull the seat frame down and slide the 1¾'' bolts into the cutouts in (D). Push the ½'' washers into the ½'' countersunk holes and tighten wing nuts (see drawing 57-3).

To fold the chairs flat, just loosen wing nuts, raise the seat, and collapse the front legs against the back legs.

Fold-up Lounge

(Photos on page 54)

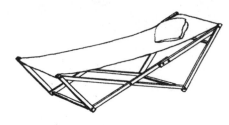

Ah yes, the joys of outdoor living: stretching out in a shady spot and snoozing away the afternoon. This lightweight folding hammock is the perfect cradle for a lazy summer day.
Design: Duane Haggerty, Pine Design

Tools you'll need:

pencil · measuring tape · square · crosscut saw or power circular saw · chisel · drill with $\frac{3}{16}''$, $\frac{3}{8}''$, $\frac{1}{2}''$, and $1\frac{3}{8}''$ bits · screwdriver · needle-nose pliers · sandpaper and finishing tools · sewing equipment and a sewing machine. *Helpful tools* include a table saw or radial-arm saw, drill press, and power sander.

Materials list

All hardware and fastenings should be rust-resistant.
36' of 1 by 2 Clear pine: 2 @ 10', 2 @ 8'
16' of rounds, $1\frac{5}{16}''$: 2 @ 8'
8 stove bolts, $\frac{3}{16}''$ by 3''
2 stove bolts, $\frac{3}{16}''$ by $2\frac{1}{4}''$
4 stove bolts, $\frac{3}{16}''$ by $1\frac{1}{2}''$
8 square nuts, $\frac{3}{16}''$
6 wing nuts, $\frac{3}{16}''$
20 washers, #10
8 fender washers, $\frac{3}{16}''$
6 flathead screws, $\frac{3}{4}''$ by #8
3 yards of 30''-wide #10 canvas
Matching cotton-wrapped polyester thread
Clear polyurethane exterior finish

Here's How

Begin by cutting to size the 1 by 2 stock, according to drawings 58-1 and 58-3. Use a square for marking and checking your cuts. Cut one (A), (E), and (F) from each 8-footer; cut one (B), (C), and (D) from each 10-footer.

Mark the 1 by 2 pieces for location of bolt holes. Note that not all holes are counterbored, and that some are counterbored on opposite sides

of the same piece. At specified locations, counterbore $\frac{1}{2}''$ holes $\frac{1}{4}''$ deep, then center a $\frac{3}{16}''$ bit in each hole and drill through. Drill remaining $\frac{3}{16}''$ holes.

Next, refer to drawing 58-2 for lengths of rounds and the placement of $\frac{3}{8}''$ and $\frac{3}{16}''$ holes in them. Drill the $\frac{3}{8}''$ holes first—about 1'' deep. Then center the $\frac{3}{16}''$ bit at the end of the round and drill straight, intersecting the $\frac{3}{8}''$ hole.

Sand the wooden parts, wipe them clean, and apply two coats of clear polyurethane finish.

Make the sling to a finished size of 100'' by 27''. Sew 1'' hems along both long edges and a casing for $1\frac{1}{4}''$ dowels at each end. For more about how to sew this type of sling, see page 76.

Insert one round (G) into one of the sling's casings, and (H) into the other; set the sling aside. Assemble the frame with 1 by 2s and the remaining rounds, as shown in drawing 58-3.

Now take the sling and, with rounds in casings, bolt (G) into place. Drape the other end of the sling over round (J) and pull down on (H) to stretch the fabric until it is fairly taut. Mark the location of (H) on both (D). These marks indicate the locations for the tension adjustment brackets (F).

Fasten (F) in place with $\frac{3}{4}''$ by #8 screws, centering the top slots of (F) over the (H) marks so that when the sling stretches with use, you can tighten it up two full notches.

To fold the lounge for storage, just remove from the (A), (B), and (C) pieces the $1\frac{1}{2}''$ and $2\frac{1}{4}''$ bolts, with wing nuts, washers, and spacers (I). Fold the head of the lounge toward the foot until flat.

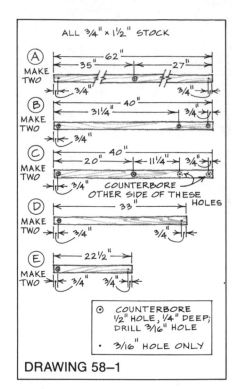

ALL 3/4" × 1/2" STOCK

DRAWING 58–1

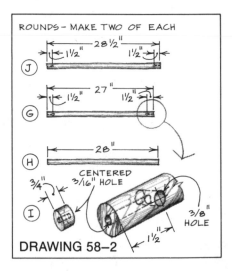

ROUNDS – MAKE TWO OF EACH

DRAWING 58–2

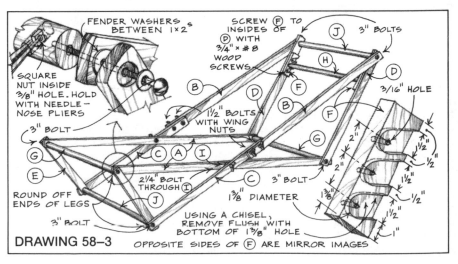

DRAWING 58–3

Work Centers

One for green-thumbers, one for chefs

Fold-away Garden Work Center

(Photos at right and on page 60)

A greenthumber's delight, this garden work center stores small garden tools, pots, soil mixes, fertilizers—all kinds of garden clutter—out of view. In addition, its fold-down door serves as a spacious work counter.

The cabinet is basically a large plywood box with shelves, dividers, and doors. Because it is heavy and awkward to move, be sure to construct it near where you'll want to use it.
Design: Donald Wm. MacDonald

Tools you'll need:

pencil · measuring tape · chalk line · protractor · T-bevel · power circular saw · drill with a $1\frac{1}{4}''$ bit · hammer · nailset (or large nail) · screwdriver · sandpaper and finishing tools. *Helpful tools* include a table saw or radial-arm saw, power sander, and paint sprayer.

Materials list

All hardware and fastenings should be rust-resistant.
5 sheets of $\frac{3}{4}''$ A-C exterior plywood, 4' by 8'
12' of 2 by 4 utility redwood
1 pound of 8d ($2\frac{1}{2}''$) finishing nails
1 dozen 4d ($1\frac{1}{2}''$) finishing nails
10 hinges, $1\frac{1}{2}''$, with screws
2 cabinet hasps
10' of lightweight chain

4 small screw eyes
Wood filler
Waterproof resorcinol glue
Primer-sealer
Exterior latex or enamel paint

Garden work center unfolds to provide handy work surface; stores garden supplies within easy reach.

(Continued on next page)

. . . Continued from page 59

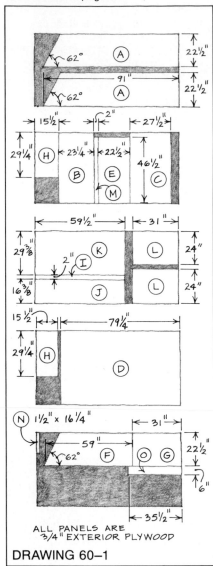

DRAWING 60–1

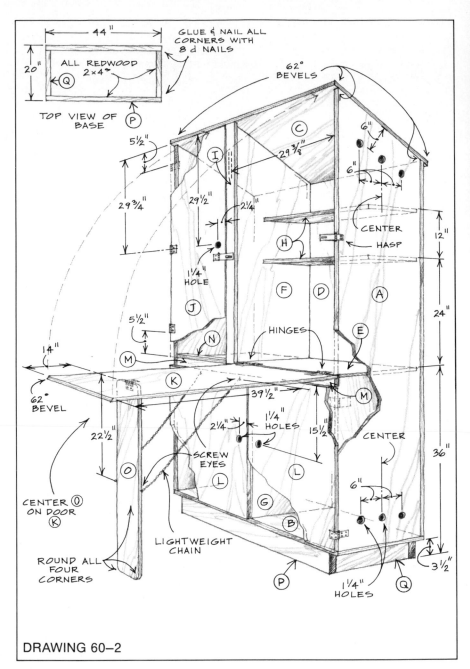

DRAWING 60–2

Garden center's counter folds away.

Here's How

Begin by measuring, marking with a pencil and chalk line, and cutting out the plywood pieces as shown in cutting diagram 60-1. Be sure to measure and cut very carefully.

Use a protractor and T-bevel to set the saw blade, and cut a 62° bevel along the long edges of (C), one short edge of (D), and what will be the top edges of (J) and (K)—refer to drawing 60-2.

Plan to build the "shell" first, then add inner dividers and shelves, doors, and so forth. For all plywood joints, use glue and 8d nails (except for those where 4d nails are specified). Nail every 6″ to 8″, setting the nail heads.

Fasten the bottom (B) to the bottom edges of the sides (A), keeping it flush at all four corners. Then glue and nail the top (C) in place (see drawing 60-2 for direction of beveled edges). Add the back (D), beveled edge upward.

Turn the cabinet onto its side and glue and nail the main horizontal shelf (E) to one side. Turn it again to glue and nail the shelf to the other side and the back. Glue and nail the main vertical divider (F) through the shelf (E) and top (C). Add a few nails from the back.

Next glue and nail the divider (G) in place, nailing through the bottom (B) and shelf (E). Add the two upper shelves (H) between the side (A) and vertical divider (F).

Screw a hasp onto (J) where shown in drawing 60-2. Also drill the $1\frac{1}{4}''$ finger holes through doors (J) and (L). Center (I) on the front edge of (F) and glue and nail in place; glue and nail (M) to the front

edge of (E). Attach door (J) to the side (A) with two hinges. Screw the remainder of the door's hasp to (I).

Hinge the fold-down door (K) onto (M) as shown in drawing 60-2. Screw the hasp parts to (A) and (K).

Hinge the bottom doors (L) to the sides (A). Then glue and nail in place with 4d nails the stop (N) for the upper door (J).

Assemble the redwood base from (P) and (Q), as shown in drawing 60-2. Spread glue along the top edge of those pieces, center the

frame on the bottom of the cabinet, and nail it through the cabinet's bottom (B) with 8d nails.

Set the unit upright and screw the leg (O) onto the fold-down door (K), positioning it as shown in the drawing. Add the two lengths of lightweight chain with screw eyes.

Fill all holes and sand the pieces smooth, slightly rounding exposed edges and corners.

Finish the cabinet with one coat of a primer-sealer and two coats of exterior latex or enamel paint.

Barbecue Center

(Photos at right and on page 62)

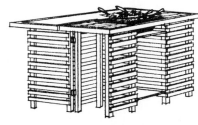

Dazzle your family and friends with this handsome barbecue center and the fantastic feasts you cook and serve on it. Two rectangular hibachis nestle in the center of the smartly tiled work surface. The cook stands at one side of the counter; guests gather at the other, where a drop leaf swings up for additional counter space.

Be advised that this project is one of the more difficult and expensive to build in this book. And be sure to buy the hibachis and tile first; as you can see in the plans, precise measurements of the counter depend upon the exact sizes of these elements.

Design: Donald Wm. MacDonald

Barbecue center has tile top, built-in hibachis.

Tools you'll need:

pencil • measuring tape • square • straightedge • crosscut saw • saber saw or keyhole saw • drill with a 1'' bit and a #10 by $1\frac{1}{2}''$ pilot bit • hammer • nailset (or large nail) • screwdriver • sandpaper and finishing tools. *Helpful tools* include a power circular saw, table saw, or radial-arm saw; backsaw and miter box; and power sander. *For laying the tile,* you'll need a tile cutter (if you don't have one, your tile dealer may loan you one or cut the tiles for you), notched trowel, and sponge.

Materials list

All hardware and fastenings should be rust-resistant.
182' of 1 by 2 pine: 6 @ 12', 7 @ 10', 2 @ 8', 4 @ 6'
36' of 2 by 2 pine: 6 @ 6'
1 sheet of $\frac{3}{4}''$ A-C exterior plywood, 4' by 8'
60 glazed ceramic tiles, approximately 4'' by 8'' by $\frac{1}{2}''$ (the actual dimensions of tile are usually smaller than the nominal dimensions to allow for grout joints)
1 pound of 4d ($1\frac{1}{2}''$) finishing nails
8 flathead screws, $1\frac{1}{2}''$ by #10

4 butt hinges, 3'', with screws
2 butt hinges, 4'', with screws
Tile mastic
Dark tile grout (optional)
Wood filler (pine)
Waterproof resorcinol glue
Polyurethane penetrating oil-sealer finish
2 hibachis, 10'' by 20''

(Continued on next page)

. . . *Continued from page 61)*

Here's How

Begin by sizing the top and cutting
its pieces. As you can see in drawing
63-1, no dimensions are given for
the countertop or drop-leaf pieces—
their sizes are determined by the
exact dimensions of the tiles you
buy. So buy the tiles first.

Lay out three rows of nineteen
tiles each, on one corner of the
plywood sheet (refer to drawing
63-1). If you plan to lay them in the
top without mastic or grout, butt
them tightly together. But if you plan
to adhere and grout them, allow
approximately $\frac{1}{4}''$ between tiles, and
between tiles and the wood rim.

Locate the outer perimeter of the
tiles on the plywood, then use a
square and straightedge to mark the
cutting lines. Measure the width to
be sure it does not exceed 24''.
Using a crosscut saw or power
circular saw, cut to the outside of the
lines. Then use this piece as a
template for marking the drop leaf;
cut it out too.

Next cut the pieces specified in
the following cutting list (refer to
drawing 63-1). Be sure to use a
square for marking and checking
your cuts. Starting with the 1 by 2s,
cut three (A) and three (B) pieces
from each of six 10-footers and the
remaining (A) and (B) pieces from
an 8-footer. From five 12-footers,
cut the (C) pieces, then five of (D).
Cut the remaining (D) pieces from
one 10-footer and one 12-footer.
Then cut (E) and (F) from the 2 by 2
stock.

(A) Twenty 1 by 2s, 20''
(B) Twenty 1 by 2s, 19$\frac{1}{4}''$
(C) Ten 1 by 2s, 62$\frac{1}{2}''$
(D) Twenty 1 by 2s, 17''
(E) Eight 2 by 2s, 35''
(F) Four 2 by 2s, 34$\frac{3}{4}''$

Set aside the remaining plywood
and lumber for later use. To assemble
the base, work in the following
sequence. Use 4d finishing nails and
waterproof glue for attaching the 1
by 2s to the 2 by 2s (two nails at
each end of each piece). Refer to
drawing 63-1 for positioning.

First, attach the (A) slats to 4 of
the (E) legs, then the (C) slats to the
remaining (E) legs. Tie the front and
back sides together by adding the
(D) slats.

Serving counter of barbecue center swings down.

Now cut two shelves from the
extra plywood, each 17'' by 24'' (if
you wish, you can cut additional
shelves from another plywood sheet).

Glue and nail one of these shelves
to the bottom slats (D), flush with the
outside edge of (C). Next, attach (B)
slats to (F) legs to make gate legs,
then fasten the gate legs to the base
with 3''-butt hinges.

Next, center the plywood top on
the base. Mark squares around the
legs where they contact the
underside of the top. Turn over the
top and drill small holes through
the plywood in the center of each
square. Reposition the top on the
base, right side up, then drill pilot
holes through the top into the legs
with a #10 by 1$\frac{1}{2}''$ pilot bit. Screw
the top in place.

Next cut the remaining 1 by 2s to
rim the countertop and drop leaf,
mitering the corners. Glue and nail
them in place with 4d nails.

Attach the drop leaf to the top with
the two 4''-butt hinges. You may need
to provide backing for hinges. The
easiest way to do this is to turn the
table upside down, aligning the two
pieces. Glue and nail pieces of
scrap plywood under the countertop
and leaf.

Next cut the hole for the hibachis.
Plan to have them project $\frac{3}{4}''$ to 1''
above the *tile*. Note that they are not
supported by the countertop—they
stand on the shelf below. This way,
the sides of the hibachis do not
contact the countertop (otherwise
they might pose a fire hazard). When
sizing the hole, allow $\frac{3}{4}''$ of air space
around the perimeter of the two
hibachis. Start by drilling a 1''-
diameter hole, then use a saber saw
or keyhole saw for cutting.

Set all nails and fill the nail holes.
Sand the entire unit and apply three
coats of polyurethane penetrating
oil-sealer to everything (except the
countertop base, if you plan to set
the tiles with mastic). Allow to dry.

Now lay out the tiles on the
countertop, spacing them so their
edges butt against the perimeter
molding. If you're laying them loose,
the tiles should fit snugly against
each other. If you're setting them in
mastic, allow for grout joints.
Around the hibachis' opening, mark

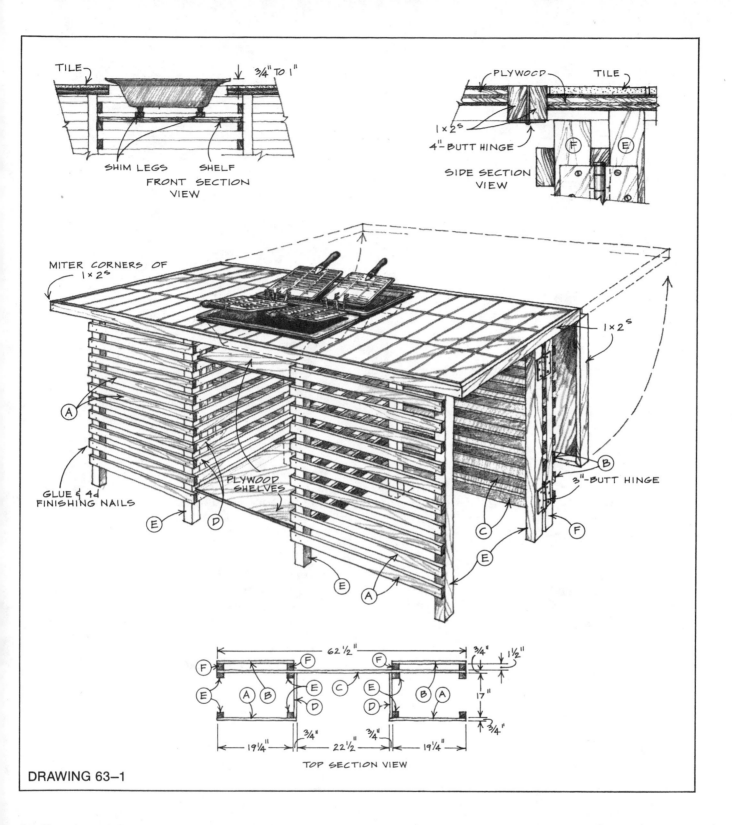

TILE   3/4" TO 1"

SHIM LEGS   SHELF
FRONT SECTION
VIEW

PLYWOOD   TILE

1 x 2s

4"-BUTT HINGE

SIDE SECTION
VIEW

F   E

MITER CORNERS OF
1 x 2s

1 x 2s

A

PLYWOOD
SHELVES

GLUE & 4d
FINISHING NAILS

E   D

E

E   A

B

3"-BUTT HINGE

C

E

F

F   F   F

E   A   B   E   C   E   B   A

E   D   D   E

62 1/2"   3/4"   1 1/2"

17"

3/4"

19 1/4"   3/4"   22 1/2"   3/4"   19 1/4"

TOP SECTION VIEW

DRAWING 63-1

the tiles where they will need to be cut to fit flush with the opening. Cut the tiles or have your dealer cut them. Set these tiles with mastic, whether or not you intend to set and grout the rest of the tiles. This will

keep the remaining tiles from shifting, if you've decided to lay them loose. (For more information on cutting and setting tile, refer to the *Sunset* book *Remodeling with Tile*.) Wipe excess grout off the surface of the tiles with a damp sponge, then let the grout set.

Slide in the top shelf between the (D) slats that are nearest to the correct height for supporting the hibachis. Then, if necessary, shim the hibachis' legs so that the rims will project 3/4" to 1" above the tile.

Materials and Techniques

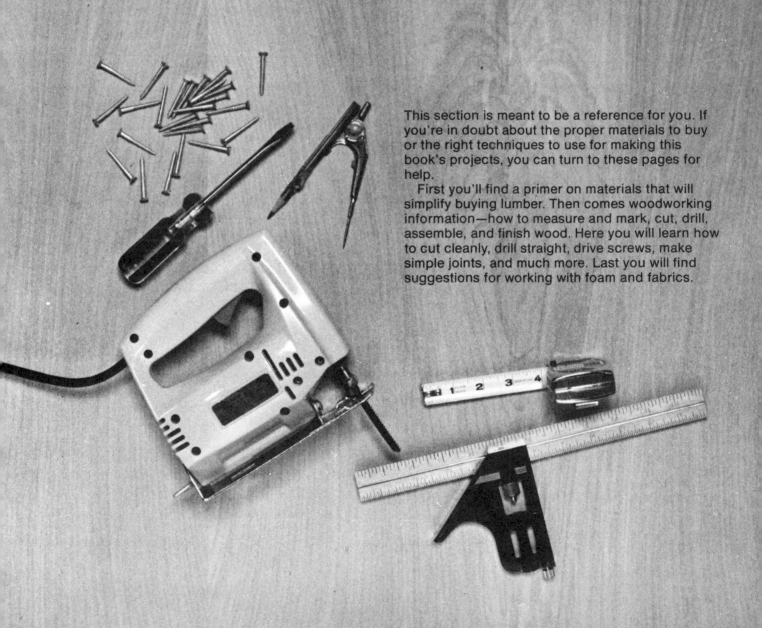

This section is meant to be a reference for you. If you're in doubt about the proper materials to buy or the right techniques to use for making this book's projects, you can turn to these pages for help.

First you'll find a primer on materials that will simplify buying lumber. Then comes woodworking information—how to measure and mark, cut, drill, assemble, and finish wood. Here you will learn how to cut cleanly, drill straight, drive screws, make simple joints, and much more. Last you will find suggestions for working with foam and fabrics.

Basics for buying lumber

You're standing at the lumberyard's checkout counter. The cash register's numbers spin madly like cherries in a slot machine. You wait with bated breath. Then it happens—the total slams into view. You lose.

It's tough to win, but the surest way to hedge your losses is to brief yourself before visiting the lumberyard. Be sure to shop around. Make a list of your requirements and call several dealers to find the best price.

Hardwood or softwood?

Wood is of two main types: hardwood and softwood. As a rule, hardwoods come from deciduous trees, softwoods from conifers. Hardwoods are usually—but not always—harder than softwoods.

Standard lumber is softwood. What we call a "1 by 4" or "2 by 4" is typically a milled length of pine, fir, redwood, cedar, spruce, or some other softwood. Because common softwoods are considerably less expensive than most hardwoods, a large majority of outdoor furniture is made from softwoods.

Species sometimes plays an important role in the selection of a wood. Redwood and cedar heartwoods have a natural resistance to decay. These species are the best to use where the wood is continually in contact with the ground or where it goes through continuous cycles of being wet and dry.

The seasoning of wood

Some lumber has been kiln-dried and some has been air-dried. Kiln-drying is a more expensive process that reduces moisture content in wood to less than 8 percent. Usually the best—and most expensive—grades of woods are kiln-dried. Though kiln-dried lumber is used primarily indoors, it is a good choice for high-quality outdoor furniture when given a protective finish.

Air-drying lumber reduces its moisture to between 12 and 20 percent. Most general construction work is done with air-dried lumber. Keep in mind that wood having this much moisture can shrink or contort as it dries further.

What quality?

Start by choosing wood that is straight and flat. Stay away from wood that is bowed, twisted, split, or warped. Beyond that, the amount of money you spend will be directly affected by the grade of wood you choose.

If you want the best, look for "Clear," "Clear All-Heart," "Supreme Finish," "Supreme," or "B and better"—the particular term depends upon the wood's species.

For wood with slight defects, watch for "Select Heart," "Select," "Prime Finish," "C-select," or "Choice." For outdoor construction not requiring particularly dry or goodlooking lumber, choose "Construction" grades.

What size?

Softwoods are sold in 2' increments, with lengths ranging from 8' to 20'. The thickness and width of a particular board depend in part upon whether it is rough or finished. (Nearly all of the projects in this book specify finished lumber—rough lumber has a very coarse, splintery texture.)

In rough lumber, the nominal dimensions are pretty close to what you get. In other words, a "2 by 4" is about 2 inches by 4 inches. But when that lumber is dried and

Standard Dimensions of Finished Lumber

SIZE TO ORDER	SURFACED (Actual Size)
1 x 2	¾" x 1½"
1 x 3	¾" x 2½"
1 x 4	¾" x 3½"
1 x 6	¾" x 5½"
1 x 8	¾" x 7¼"
1 x 10	¾" x 9¼"
1 x 12	¾" x 11¼"
2 x 3	1½" x 2½"
2 x 4	1½" x 3½"
2 x 6	1½" x 5½"
2 x 8	1½" x 7¼"
2 x 10	1½" x 9¼"
2 x 12	1½" x 11¼"

Thickness of 3" lumber is 2½" and of 4" lumber is 3½".

surfaced, as is done with all finished lumber, it ends up considerably short of the 2" and 4" dimensions. A finished 2 by 4 is actually 1½" by 3½". Other nominal and actual sizes are shown in the chart (below, left).

Hardwood lumber is normally sold in odd lengths and sizes by the lineal foot, board foot, or even by the pound. When you need hardwood for a particular project, specify the footage you need and ask the salesperson to sell you what is in stock that will fill your requirements with the least waste. Again, hand pick your lumber if possible.

What about plywood?

Plywood has several advantages over lumber: exceptional strength, high resistance to warp, availability in large sheets, and, in most cases, lower cost.

Plywood comes in a range of thicknesses: ⅛", ³⁄₁₆", ¼", ⅜", ½", ⅝", ¾". Standard sheets are 4' by 8'.

Plywood, like lumber, falls into two categories: softwood and hardwood. In the case of plywood, the difference lies in the species of wood used for the outer faces of a panel.

Softwood plywoods are most commonly used for outdoor construction. Typically, these are fir, cedar, or redwood (the cedar and redwood plywoods are manufactured as house siding). In the hardwood category, birch-veneered plywood is a good selection. Handsome, light toned, and durable, it is one of the lowest-priced hardwood plywoods. Ash is another good low-cost hardwood plywood choice.

Plywood is graded according to the quality of the veneers on both sides. "A-A" is the best; use it only where the appearance of both sides is important. "A-B," "A-C," and "A-D" have a high-quality veneer on the face and a lower-quality veneer on the back. "C-C" and "C-D" are rough construction grades, but you can get a "plugged C-D" panel with one face that has been patched and sanded and is quite suitable for painting. Softwood panels may be interior or exterior type—be sure to buy panels marked "Exterior" for outdoor use.

How to measure and mark

Most important in starting a project properly are careful measuring and marking. These first woodworking steps will set the stage for your finished project. By precise measuring and marking, you can avoid wasting time and materials and take the first step toward professional-looking results.

For most projects, you'll use a pencil, a measuring tape, and a combination square. For some projects, you'll also need a yardstick and a compass.

MEASURING AND MARKING TOOLS

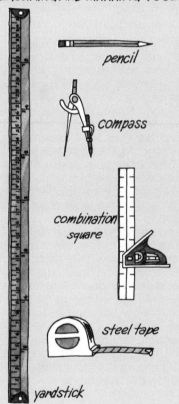

pencil

compass

combination square

steel tape

yardstick

Measuring. Tight-fitting joinery requires measuring and cutting to within $\frac{1}{32}$" or $\frac{1}{64}$," use a yard-stick, a metal tape measure, or the blade of a square. A tape measure's end hook should be riveted loosely so that it slides the distance of its

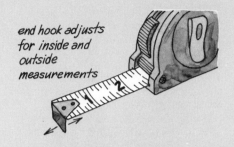

end hook adjusts for inside and outside measurements

own thickness, adjusting for precise "inside" and "outside" measurements.

Because measuring is easy and most materials are expensive, it pays to double-check your measurements. And whenever possible during construction, transfer measurements directly from one material to another rather than measuring again.

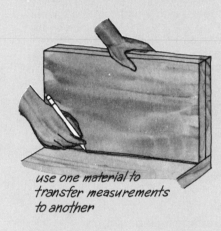

use one material to transfer measurements to another

Marking lines. A sharp pencil works well for drawing lines. Draw straight lines by guiding the pencil along the edge of a square or straightedge. Use a compass to draw curves or small circles.

For drawing large circles—such as the top for a round table—tack one end of a yardstick to the

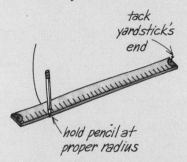

tack yardstick's end

hold pencil at proper radius

material's center and, holding the pencil at the proper radius, turn the yardstick like a large clock hand.

For marking straight across a board at 90° or at 45,° use a combination square.

Checking for square. Use a combination square for this purpose. Depending upon which side of the square's handle you use, you can check for a true 90° or 45° angle.

Place the handle of the square firmly along one of the board's side surfaces, sliding the blade into contact with the board end. If light shows between the blade and the board, the end is not true. Check across both the width and the thickness of the board. Plane or sand the ridges until the edge is square and no light shows through.

checking board's end for square

checking 45° miter

checking inside for square

Cutting wood

In furniture making, your cuts must be precise. They should be clean, square, and straight (unless they're supposed to be angled or curved). When you join two pieces, no gaps should show between them.

For proper cutting, you need the right tools. What are the "right tools"? That depends upon the project.

Cutting tools range from the simple and inexpensive to the sophisticated and costly. Generally speaking, hand tools are considerably less expensive than power tools. But some power tools—such as saber saws and electric drills—come in inexpensive models that cost little more than their hand-powered counterparts. A saber saw greatly simplifies cutting both straight lines and curves in materials as thick as 1".

Some projects require sophisticated tools, but there may be ways of getting around buying them. Following are three alternatives.

• You can have cuts made at the lumberyard. Most lumberyards make straight cuts for a small fee. If you decide to do this, have the yard make the longest cuts. But before you do, find out how much the cutting costs and whether or not it can be done precisely.

• You can join an adult education woodworking class. In many localities, high schools and colleges offer night classes on woodworking. These schools usually have excellent tools and very helpful instructors.

• One other alternative is to look up "Cabinet Makers" in the Yellow Pages and call two or three for cost estimates on doing procedures you are not equipped for. You'll probably have to take your plans in to get firm estimates.

Miscellaneous cutting tools. Though they don't fit the category of saws, tools such as chisels, planes, files, and the router are designed for cutting.

Chisels are used primarily for notching and cutting grooves (see "How to cut grooves" on page 68). They come in several sizes.

Planes slice off unwanted portions of wood, controlling the width and depth of their cut. A block plane—the short one—cuts end grain well. A jack plane, about twice the length of a block plane, shears bumps and irregularities off a board's edges.

Abrasive tools, such as files and rasps, remove small quantities of wood and make small areas smooth. They come in many shapes, sizes, and degrees of coarseness.

A router is versatile—it grooves, shaves, bevels, and rounds wood, depending upon the bit used. This

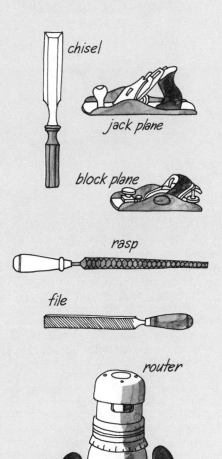

chisel

jack plane

block plane

rasp

file

router

power tool cuts straight grooves, V-shaped grooves, rounded grooves, and even exact dovetails. It can round or bevel the edge of a board in a single pass. Though rather expensive, a router can give projects a very finished look.

How to make a clean cut. The number of teeth per inch along a saw blade determines the kind of cut it makes. The more numerous the teeth, the smoother the cut. Choose a blade with 10 to 12 teeth per inch. For cutting plywood smoothly with power saws, various kinds of blades are available.

Wood tends to splinter and break away where saw teeth exit. The kind of saw you use will determine the side of the wood on which this happens. Some saws have upward-cutting blades; others cut downward. If you're not sure, look to see which direction the teeth point—that's the direction that saw cuts.

Cut with the good side up when using a handsaw, table saw, or radial-arm saw. If you use a portable circular saw or saber saw, cut the wood good-side-down. To minimize splintering, score along the backside of the cutting line. Or try taping the line's backside with masking tape. Better yet, back the cut by pressing or clamping a scrap against the piece you're cutting and cut both pieces together.

Don't forget to support both halves of the piece you're cutting. Otherwise the saw will bind and, as you near the end of the cut, the unsupported piece will break away. If the saw binds anyway, stick a screwdriver blade in the end of the cut to spread it open.

Sawing straight lines. Several kinds of saws can cut straight lines: handsaw, saber saw, power circular saw, table saw, and radial-arm saw. The right method for cutting straight depends upon the saw you use.

The secret of cutting straight is using a guide. Table saws and radial-arm saws have built-in guides, but if you use a hand-held saw, you'll have to improvise a guide or use a small guide attachment.

(Continued on page 68)

. . . Continued from page 67

Guide a handsaw against a board clamped along the cutting line. Start a cut by drawing the saw slowly *up* a few times to make a

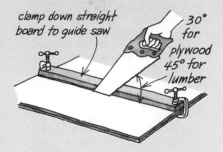

clamp down straight board to guide saw

30° for plywood 45° for lumber

notch or "kerf." Making a full kerf about ½" into the board's far edge will help to guide the blade straight for the rest of the cut. Then saw with short strokes at the blade's wide end, progressing to smooth, long, generous strokes. Keep your forearm in line with the blade as you work. Saw lumber at a 45° angle; cut plywood and other sheet materials at 30°.

A saber saw usually comes with a guide designed for making straight cuts a short distance from, and parallel to, a board's edge. When cutting across panels or wide surfaces, guide the saw's base plate against a straightedge clamped a measured distance from the cutting line. Keep the saw firmly against the guide and check the blade continually to see that it doesn't bend away from the cut; it should stay vertically straight. Wear eye protection when using a saber saw.

Power circular saws also come with guides for ripping narrow widths. For cutting large panels, make a reusable guide from scrap plywood and molding as shown below. Work carefully and wear eye protection.

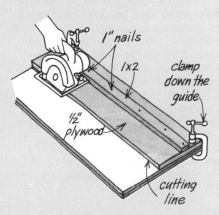

1" nails

1x2

clamp down the guide

½" plywood

cutting line

Sawing curves and irregular lines. Blades for sawing curves, zigzags, or irregular cuts must be thin and narrow. They are used in an almost straight-up-and-down position. Saws suitable for this kind of cutting are the keyhole saw, coping saw, and saber saw.

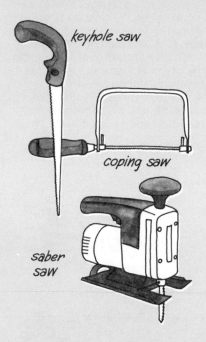

keyhole saw

coping saw

saber saw

The keyhole saw is the hand-powered version of the saber saw. With it you can cut curves and make cutouts in the center of panels, but you must start it from a drilled hole.

The coping saw, limited by its metal frame, cuts tightly curved lines close to a board's edge. Its blade is removable. When cutting vertically in a vise, point the teeth toward the handle and cut on the pull stroke. When working on something supported horizontally, point the teeth away from the handle and cut on the push stroke.

The saber saw can do almost any kind of cutting. A great general purpose tool, it tracks curved lines easily. For greatest control, get a saber saw with a variable-speed trigger.

How to make a cutout. Using a saber saw, you can dip into a panel's center to make a cutout by tilting the saw forward on its toe plate, starting the motor, and slowly lowering the tool. Do this with care, wearing eye protection.

You can also make a cutout by drilling a hole about 1" in diameter, then using this hole to start a cut with a keyhole saw. Once you have cut a few inches, you can finish a long cut with a regular handsaw.

How to cut a miter. A miter is simply a through cut made at an angle—usually 45° Mark the miter first, using a combination square; then cut it just as you would cut straight across the board, but holding the saw at a slightly flatter angle. Use a fine-toothed saw and cut to the outside of the cutting line.

A great aid for cutting miters is a miter box. It supports small material securely and guides the saw for precise cuts.

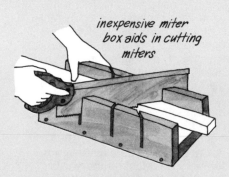

inexpensive miter box aids in cutting miters

Radial-arm saws and table saws are excellent for cutting precise miters.

How to cut grooves. Grooves are probably the most difficult kind of cuts to make, especially using hand tools. The trick is to cut a wide groove with a flat base.

Power tools cut grooves easily. The best tools are routers and power saws equipped with dado blades. You simply guide them across the surface—the bits or blades do all the work. Or, using a power saw with a regular blade, you can make a series of joined cuts within the area to be removed.

To cut a groove using hand tools, first mark the groove; then saw to the inside of the lines as deep as you want the groove. If it's a very wide cut, saw several extra cuts across the waste wood in the middle. Then use a chisel to remove the waste wood.

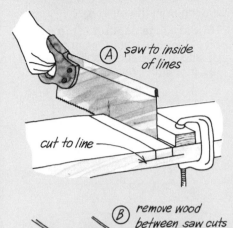

Ⓐ saw to inside of lines

cut to line

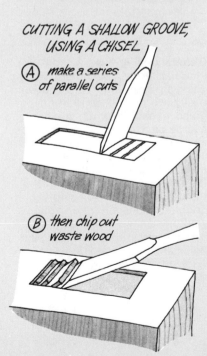

Ⓑ remove wood between saw cuts

chisel

If the groove doesn't extend to the board's edges, cut it with a chisel. Lightly rap the chisel with a hammer on each cross-grain mark

CUTTING A SHALLOW GROOVE, USING A CHISEL

Ⓐ make a series of parallel cuts

Ⓑ then chip out waste wood

(with the bevel facing waste wood) to keep the wood from splitting beyond those marks. Then make a series of parallel cuts to the desired depth, moving the blade's bevel forward. Keep the chisel almost perpendicular to the surface.

Next, using the chisel without the hammer and decreasing its angle considerably, chip out all the waste wood. Make final smoothing cuts with the chisel's bevel almost flat against the wood.

For a deep groove, first remove excess wood by drilling a series of holes. Then join the holes and square up the resulting mortise with a chisel.

MAKING A DEEP GROOVE (MORTISE)

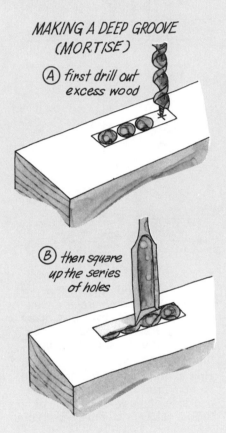

Ⓐ first drill out excess wood

Ⓑ then square up the series of holes

How to cut slots. Several of this book's projects consist of panels joined by interlocking joints. In the joinery section of this book, on page 74, you'll learn how to make an interlocking joint. Such a joint requires that you cut a slot in each panel. Cutting this kind of slot is a simple job if you know how.

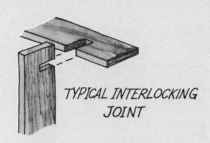

TYPICAL INTERLOCKING JOINT

Here's how:

Mark for the cuts as described in the joinery section, using a square. When you cut, be sure to cut to the *waste* side of the cutting lines. Remember, too, that it's better to remove too little wood than too much—you can always take off a little more, but adding wood is another story.

One way to cut a slot is to begin by drilling a hole the same diameter as the slot's width, located at the end of the slot. Then cut from the panel's

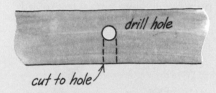

drill hole

cut to hole

edge to the hole. If necessary, square off the rounded end, using a saber saw, keyhole saw, or file.

You can also cut a slot with a saber saw or a coping saw, as shown below.

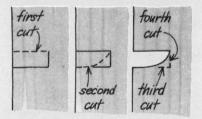

first cut

second cut

third cut

fourth cut

If you don't have a saber saw or a coping saw, you can cut a slot with a handsaw and chisel, as described under the heading "How to cut grooves," facing page.

Drilling straight, clean holes

For many of this book's projects, you'll need a drill. Though hand drills can do most of the work, a ¼" or ⅜" power drill is highly recommended. For one thing, it makes the job of drilling much faster and easier; for another, with an abundance of available attachments, it can become one of the most useful tools in your tool box.

Four drilling problems crop up often: 1) Centering the moving drill bit on its mark; 2) Drilling a hole straight; 3) Keeping the wood's backside from breaking away as the drill bit pierces; and 4) Drilling to a measured depth and knowing when to stop. The following techniques will help you deal with these problems.

How to center the bit. Keep a pointed tool handy for center punching. A couple of taps with a hammer on a large nail, nailset, or punch will leave a hole to prevent the bit from wandering.

punch a hole to keep drill bit from wandering

How to drill straight. A drill press or a press accessory for your hand drill offers the best means for drilling holes straight. But if you don't have one of these, try one of

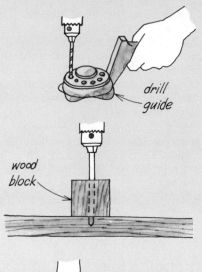

drill guide

wood block

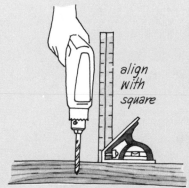

align with square

the three methods shown above. You can use a commercially available drill guide for twist bits, make a guide by predrilling a scrap block of wood, or use a square to align the drill visually.

How to drill cleanly. To keep a drill bit from breaking out through the backside of the wood, do one of two things: 1) Lay or clamp a wood scrap

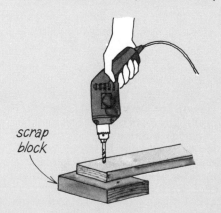

scrap block

firmly against the backside of your workpiece and drill through the workpiece into the scrap; or 2) Just after the drill's point pierces, flop the workpiece over and finish drilling from the other side.

How to gauge depth. To stop a drill bit at the right depth, wrap a piece of tape around the shank to signal the proper boring depth.

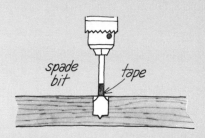

spade bit   tape

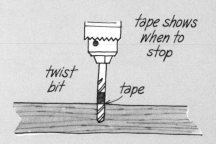

tape shows when to stop

twist bit   tape

General drilling tips. Clamp materials down, particularly when using a power drill. The torque can easily wrench the wood from your grasp, especially when you're using a large bit. Hold the drill firmly, leaving the motor on until you have withdrawn the bit from the wood. To avoid breaking small bits, don't tilt the drill once the bit has entered the wood. Wear plastic safety goggles, especially when your workpiece has a brittle surface.

For information on drilling pilot holes and countersinking, see "How to drive screws," page 72.

Fastening and joinery techniques

After you have marked, cut, and drilled pieces, the next logical step is joinery—fastening the pieces together to form a finished project. Though wood can be cut to form dozens of kinds of joints, the methods of fastening those joints are few: gluing and clamping, nailing, screwing, and bolting. This section tells how to use fasteners and how to make basic joints. For outdoor use, be sure to choose rust-resistant fasteners.

Basic fastening tools are shown at right. They are all relatively inexpensive hand tools. Of course, a saw is needed for cutting most types of joints; saws are discussed on page 67 under "Cutting wood."

Gluing and clamping. One of the best fasteners for permanent joints is glue. Glue strengthens almost all joints. Unless you use contact cement or epoxy (depending upon what you are gluing), you should clamp the joint after applying glue. C-clamps, bar clamps, or pipe clamps will handle most standard clamping jobs.

Most projects in this book specify resorcinol glue. Completely waterproof and extremely strong, it is a two-part glue that you make up by mixing a resin with a catalyst. Spread it on the adjoining surfaces, clamp or fasten them tightly together, wipe off the excess, and let dry according to label recommendations. Don't fail to wipe off the excess—most stains and transparent finishes will not take to glue-coated areas. Be sure to follow all label directions.

Choose and use other kinds of glue according to their labels.

C-clamps work well for miscellaneous clamping jobs. They come in various sizes, with openings from 3" to 16". Protect wooden surfaces from damage from a metal clamp's jaws by slipping a scrap block between the jaws and the wood before you tighten the clamp.

Bar clamps and pipe clamps work well for clamping across broad surfaces. Bar clamps open as far as the bar part of the clamp allows. Pipe clamps depend for their maximum spread upon the length of pipe you attach them to.

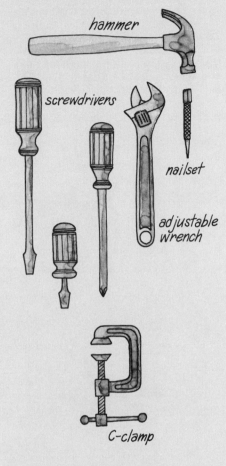

hammer

screwdrivers

nailset

adjustable wrench

C-clamp

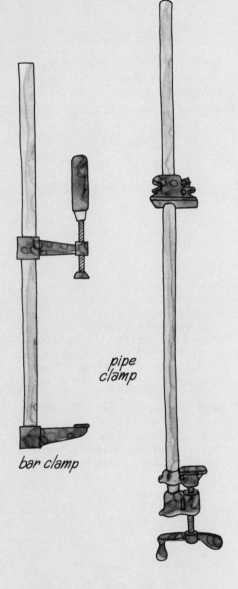

pipe clamp

bar clamp

How to nail. Nailing is easy, inexpensive, and fast. It works fine where only medium strength is needed—but use glue too. Never expect nails to hold a chair's primary joints or other joints where they might work loose.

Nails with sharp points hold better than blunt ones, but they tend to split wood. Before driving a nail into wood that splits easily,

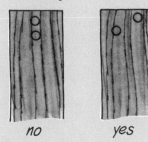

don't line up nails along same grain line

no   yes

blunt the point with a tap of the hammer (or predrill nail holes). And don't line up two nails along the same grain lines in the board— the wood will probably split if you do. Instead, stagger nails slightly.

When starting a nail, hold it near its head. That way, if you miss, you'll only knock your fingers away. Once the nail is started, let go of it and swing the hammer with fuller strokes, hitting the nail's head squarely. Keep the hammer's

keep hammer's face
perpendicular with nail head
upon contact

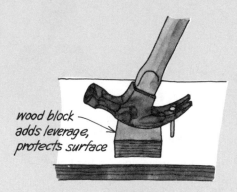

use nailset to sink
nails below
surface

face perpendicular to the nail head upon contact.

Where you are concerned about the wood's appearance, be very careful not to crush the surface with the last few hammer blows. If you wish to camouflage the nails, use a nailset to set the nails below the surface about ⅛"; then fill the holes with wood filler.

When pulling a nail, put a scrap block under the hammer's head so you won't damage the surface of the wood.

wood block
adds leverage,
protects surface

How to drive screws. Though screws are slightly more difficult and time consuming to drive than nails, they are considerably stronger, especially when supplemented with glue. Screws used without glue can be removed, creating a joint that can be taken apart.

Drill pilot holes for screws. Either select a drill bit slightly smaller than the screw's shank or use a "pilot bit." As shown in the drawing below,

pilot bit drills
exact hole
for screw

①

②

③

this bit drills a hole that's just the right shape for a particular screw. Some bits are adjustable; others match a particular screw size. The latter type is the more reliable.

When screwing into end grain, it's a good idea first to drill a hole and insert a hardwood dowel perpendicular to the path of the screw.

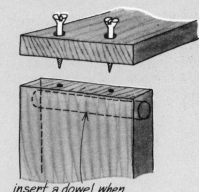

insert a dowel when
screwing into end grain

This gives the screw something strong to grip.

Be sure to use a screwdriver that fits the screw's slot, not one that's too small or too large. And don't work with a burred or bent screwdriver.

If you don't want screw heads to show, countersink them below the wood's surface; then fill the hole above the head with putty or with a wooden plug. To use a wooden plug, drill the countersinking hole from ⅛" to ⅜" deep and, instead of doweling, use a "plug-cutter" bit to cut the plug from a scrap of the same wood. This way, the grain and color of the plug will match that of the wood you're plugging.

How to use bolts. Unlike a screw, which digs into wood, a bolt has a threaded shaft that grips a nut. Because it grips the nut rather than the wood, a bolt is very strong and doesn't chew up the wood when removed.

Several types of bolts are available, with various kinds of heads. Some you tighten with a screwdriver,

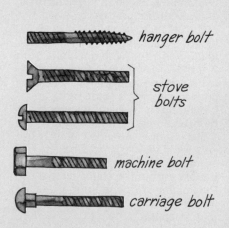

hanger bolt

stove
bolts

machine bolt

carriage bolt

others with a wrench. You drive a hanger bolt by running two nuts on the shaft, tightening them together, and then driving the top nut with a wrench.

You can countersink a bolt head the same way you'd countersink a screw (see "How to drive screws," facing page). But if you plan to plug or fill over the bolt's head, yet you want to be able to disassemble the parts, you should use carriage bolts. They permit disassembly without the use of a tool on the bolt's head.

Several kinds of nuts are available. The kinds most commonly used are hex nuts, acorn nuts, wing

hex nut   square nut

wing nut   T-nut

acorn ("cap") nut

nuts, and T-nuts. T-nuts fit flush on a surface and provide metal threads in a hole. A T-nut is strong only when pulled from the side of the hole opposite its body—it can't withstand a pull from the same side.

How to make a butt joint. Measure the pieces and mark them with a 90° square. Cut them carefully so there won't be gaps. Add glue and clamps and/or fasteners such as screws, nails, or dowels.

TYPICAL BUTT JOINTS

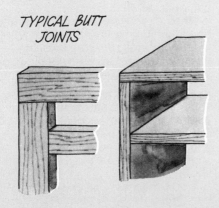

How to make a miter joint. Measure the pieces, remembering that both must go the full distance to the corner. Mark them, using a 45°

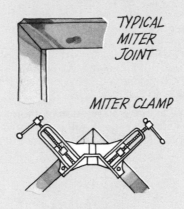

TYPICAL MITER JOINT

MITER CLAMP

HOW TO IMPROVISE A MITER CLAMP

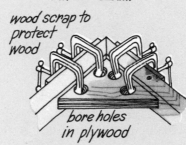

wood scrap to protect wood

bore holes in plywood

angle, and cut carefully. Apply glue to the two joining surfaces and clamp, using a special clamp made for this purpose or improvising one as shown above. Add fasteners for strength.

How to make a dowel joint. You'll encounter two different kinds of dowel joints; one is quite easy to make, but the other is more difficult, requiring special tools and careful drilling.

The first type involves cutting a basic butt joint, joining the two pieces by holding or clamping them together, and drilling holes *through* one and into the other. Next, you score small grooves along the dowels so glue can escape the holes. Then you coat the dowels and the two meeting surfaces with glue, and pound the dowels in from the outside.

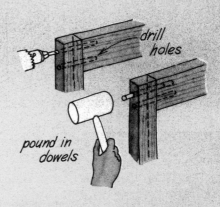

drill holes

pound in dowels

The other method, perhaps more common, is blind doweling. With this method the dowels don't show. Instead, you mark and drill separate,

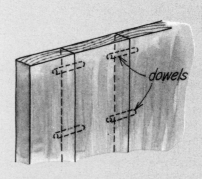

dowels

matching holes in the two meeting halves, add glue, push dowels into one of the halves, and then fit the two halves together.

doweling jig aids in drilling dowel holes

The tough part is getting the holes to match exactly and drilling them straight (see page 70). A tool called a "doweling jig" is made especially for this purpose. Clamp this tool onto one of the surfaces and drill through the guide holes. Then clamp the adjoining surface in place, unclamp the first piece, and drill the matching holes in the second surface.

Or you can mark the two pieces as shown below. Do your best to drill the holes straight (see page 70).

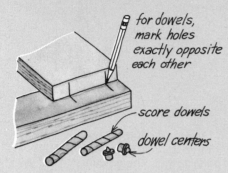

for dowels, mark holes exactly opposite each other

score dowels

dowel centers

You can also use "dowel centers." To do this, drill the holes in one surface, put the centers in the holes, and push the other piece in place against the first one. The dowel centers mark the exact place to drill.

Before pounding in dowels, cut them slightly shorter than the combined depth of the matching holes. Then score them and spread glue along them. Insert the dowels, put the two halves together, and clamp the joint tight.

How to make a spline joint. Inserting a wooden spline in a saw kerf is a simple way to strengthen miter and butt joints.

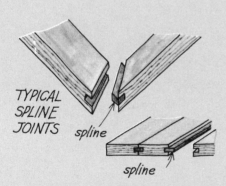

TYPICAL SPLINE JOINTS

spline

spline

spline

To be sure the grooves match, use the same table saw or router setting to cut them. The width of the spline should be slightly less than the combined depth of the kerfs. For most work, a good spline size is ¼" thick by 1¼" wide. For this, you'd cut a groove ¼" wide and about $1\frac{1}{16}$" deep in each meeting piece.

Cut the spline, spread glue along it, and put it in place in one of the grooves. Then push the other half in place and clamp.

How to make an interlocking joint. The simple slide-together joints shown below are used for several of

INTERLOCKING JOINTS

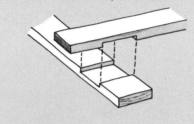

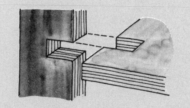

this book's projects. Flat interlocking joints between boards may require fasteners, but long-slot interlocking joints for plywood panels—those used in the furniture on page 50, for example—work well without fasteners. And you can disassemble them simply by sliding them apart.

To make them, cut matching grooves in the two pieces. The width of each groove should be exactly the same as that of the connecting piece. Normally, grooves are cut so that their point of intersection is about at the midline of each piece.

When marking for grooves, use the joining piece as a guide. Cut the grooves as explained under "How to cut grooves" and "How to cut slots" on pages 68 and 69.

Finishing wood

Wood should be given a finish to protect it from being soiled, stained, dented, or damaged by weather. A finish can also enhance the appearance of most woods. Before you apply a finish, prepare the wood by filling holes and imperfections and sanding it smooth.

Filling holes. Before filling wood, consider the finish you plan to apply. Don't use a filler that's going to stick out like a sore thumb. Of course, if you plan to paint the project, practically any filler will work—the paint should cover all.

For natural finishes, fill blemishes with wood dough or stick shellac (a specialty product for furniture makers). Both products come in colors that match most woods.

Spread wood dough with a putty knife; melt stick shellac into the hole or crack. Always build up the patch slightly above the surface and then sand off the excess. To patch a large hole, fill the hole, let the compound dry, sand the surface on and around the patch, and then repeat the process.

When you plan to stain the wood, you should use a slightly different treatment. Because dried fillers don't have the same porosity as woods, they often show up under stains—the stain gets absorbed unevenly. So choose a wood dough that is close to the wood's finished color and apply it *after* the stain.

You can touch up with stain if necessary, and then apply a finish coat of clear polyurethane. First test the color match on an extra piece of wood. You'll find that dark stains and opaque stains usually camouflage fillers best.

Whether you're applying a natural finish, staining, or painting, seal any knots with shellac before finishing—this will prevent sap from seeping through.

Sanding wood. Though sanding is sometimes a tedious job, it can give your project a professional touch. So don't neglect it—after working hard at making a project, you shouldn't scrimp on the part that shows the most.

A power sander makes sanding easy, but unless you have a large

CHARACTERISTICS OF COMMON FINISHES

	Advantages	Disadvantages	General traits
CLEAR FINISHES			
Penetrating resin	Easiest of all finishes to apply. Gives wood a natural, no-finish look.	Provides little surface protection from heat and abrasion.	Soaks into wood pores rather than coating the surface. Darkens wood grain.
Polyurethane	Simple to apply by brush. Tough. Alcohol, heat, and water resistant.	Dries slowly. Sanding is required between coats. Can't be used over many other surface finishes.	Protects wood with thick surface coating. Enhances wood grain with slight darkening effect.
Shellac	Very fast drying. Easy to thin and apply. Very tough. Will not mar or scratch easily.	Alcohol, ammonia, and detergent dissolve it. Water will turn it white unless finish is waxed often.	Multiple coats lie on the wood surface and provide a slightly amber-tinted finish.
Lacquer	Primes, seals, and finishes all in one step. Very resistant to alcohol, chemicals, heat, abrasion.	Because it is extremely fast drying, you must work quickly. Can be used only over bare wood or other lacquer.	Protects wood with thin layer of surface coating. Available for both spraying and brushing.
STAINS			
Pigmented oil stain	Simple to wipe on and off with a rag. Useful for making one wood species look like another in color.	Too pigmented to use on many fine furniture woods—often obscures pores and grain.	Colors are nonfading, nonbleeding, and available ready-mixed in a wide variety of hues.
Penetrating oil stain	Not pigmented, so pores and grain are revealed. Similar to a penetrating resin, only with color added.	Penetrates irregularly on softwoods and plywoods. Not good for making one wood look like another.	Soaks into wood rather than coating it. Colors by means of dyes rather than pigments.
Water stain	Colors are brilliant, warm toned, clear, permanent. Stain thins easily and cleans up with water.	The wood fibers are swelled by the water, making light resanding necessary. Very slow drying and difficult to apply without experience.	Stain is available in powdered dye form that you mix with water. Wood fibers are colored by the dye in the same way that a piece of cloth is dyed.
Non-grain-raising (alcohol) stain	Cool-toned, transparent colors. Rapid drying may be useful if you have many projects to do. Good for use on hardwoods only.	Very short drying time makes it difficult to use. Best when sprayed. Not for use on softwoods or plywoods.	Available in ready-mixed colors and in powdered form.
ENAMELS			
Oil-base enamel	Durable, washable, good adhesion, covers surface well.	Slow drying. Mineral spirits are required for thinning and cleanup.	Totally hides wood. All colors available in gloss, semi-gloss, and flat.
Latex enamel	Dries quickly. Thins and cleans up easily with water.	Less durability and coverage than oil-base enamels.	Totally hides wood. All colors available in semigloss and flat.

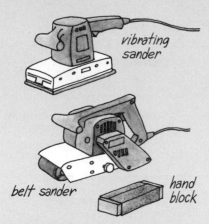

vibrating sander

belt sander

hand block

amount of sanding to do, you won't need one. Though hand sanding takes elbow grease, it produces a fine finish.

If you have one, a belt sander can remove a lot of wood fast. Use it only *in line* with the wood's grain. Graduate from coarse to fine sanding belts, but be careful—a belt sander with a coarse belt can devour your project.

Vibrating sanders work more like hand sanding. Some move the sandpaper in an "orbiting" motion; others move it back and forth. For final sanding use only the kind that works back and forth, and keep the movement in the same direction as the wood's grain.

Whether you sand by hand or power, divide the process into three steps: rough, preparatory (after you've filled defects), and finish. Rough-sand with 80-grit sandpaper; preparatory-sand with 120-grit; and finish-sand with 180-grit or finer. A final hand sanding usually improves the appearance of a finish. Prior to finishing, remove dust, using a rag moistened with mineral spirits.

Applying the finish. Many projects in this book recommend poly-urethane as a finish. Available both clear and pigmented, it is durable and easy to apply.

Three kinds of polyurethane are available: gloss, satin, and pene-trating oil-sealer. Gloss and satin lie on the surface, giving it a plastic-coated appearance. Gloss, of course, is shinier than satin. Pene-trating oil-sealer soaks into the wood, protecting it from within. Choose this kind for maximum highlighting of wood texture. No matter which type you buy, be sure it's rated for outdoor use.

Hundreds of varnishes, lacquers, oils, stains, enamels, and other finishes are available. Find out more about these from your dealer.

For a few of this book's projects, you'll need some basic know-how in working with fabrics and stuffings. This section offers basic sewing information and shows how to stuff and stitch cushions.

How to stitch a finished edge. Where fabric will be seen from both sides—the sling on the back of a chair, for example—finish the edges so they won't fray. To do this, first fold under ¼", then fold under another ¼", then pin. Stitch along the resulting triple thickness.

How to sew a loop. A small loop along a fabric edge is called a casing. With some projects you push a drawstring through this loop; in others, the loop holds a dowel or some other wooden frame member.

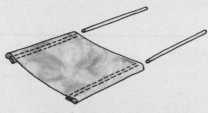

SLING WITH DOWEL CASING AT EACH END

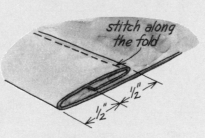

stitch along the fold

½" ½" ½"

DETAIL OF CASING FOR A DRAWSTRING

Make a casing by figuring the necessary loop size, plus ½", folding over the end to create the loop, tucking the unfinished fabric edge under about ½", and stitching along the fold. Choose heavy-duty thread and double-stitch for strength.

To make a large loop of fabric, join the two ends with a flat-fell seam. To do this, sew the two pieces together about ⅝" from their ends.

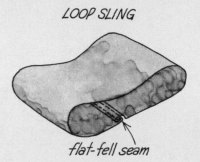

LOOP SLING

flat-fell seam

Press the joined ends down to one side; then trim the lower seam allowance to ¼". Curl the top seam allowance under it about ⅛" and pin. Topstitch it close to the fold; then turn it right side up and topstitch close to the seam for added strength.

Cushion stuffings

A cushion is generally a fabric bag filled with something soft—usually polyurethane foam or foam rubber. Some cushions have foam cores wrapped with one or more layers of polyester batting (a thick, fluffy fabric).

For each of the cushions described in this book's projects, we've recommended a particular stuffing. The various stuffings are discussed here; you can vary a stuffing, depending upon the appearance and comfort you want the cushion to have.

Foam blocks. Most firm, flat, squared-off cushions have one-piece or layered foam-block fillings. Foam blocks come in thicknesses of 1″ increments. They are sold by the square foot. Price depends upon the size, the density, the amount of cutting necessary, and, most of all, the type of foam. There are two kinds: polyurethane foam ("polyfoam") and foam rubber.

Polyfoam is much cheaper than foam rubber but lacks durability, breaking down in sunlight and with use. Foam rubber weighs more. Both come in four densities: super-soft, soft, medium, and dense. Foam rubber tends to be firmer than polyfoam in the same classification: a "soft" foam rubber is usually about the same density as a "medium" polyfoam.

Most cushions are made up of foams of two or more densities. A seat cushion, for example, commonly has a medium or dense foam core sandwiched between two outer layers (about 1″ thick) of soft foam. A typical back cushion is made the same way, but its outer layers are of super-soft foam. Additionally, cushions with a soft, rounded look are usually wrapped with at least one layer of batting.

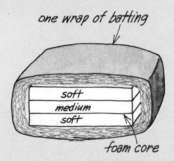

one wrap of batting

soft
medium
soft

foam core

TYPICAL SEAT CUSHION STUFFING

Buy precut blocks at large yardage stores or upholstery supply shops. For custom sizes or styles, visit an upholstery shop or a foam dealer. To find foam dealers, look in the Yellow Pages under "Rubber—Foam & Sponge."

Working with foam is easy. Use a serrated bread knife or, even better, an electric carving knife to cut it. For maximum cutting ease, spray the knife's blade with silicone or a nonstick vegetable coating. To glue foam pieces together, buy from a foam dealer an easy-to-use foam adhesive made for the purpose.

Foam bolsters and pillows. Polyfoam and foam rubber also come in precut pillow forms and in cylindrical bolsters. Bolsters are sold by foam density and by diameter and length.

Shredded foam. The easiest form of cushion stuffing to obtain—shredded foam—is sold in yardage, notions, and variety stores. Basically, it is the same foam discussed under "Foam blocks," chopped into small chunks by a shredder. Shredded foam is cheap and easy to stuff into a fabric form; but those are practically its only virtues. It looks and feels lumpy, doesn't hold a particular shape, and is messy. If you plan to stuff a cushion with shredded foam, consider making an inner bag of muslin so you can remove the cover easily for cleaning.

Polyester batting. This synthetic has the feel of fluffy cotton. In cushion making, it's most commonly wrapped around foam blocks to soften and round them. For this purpose it's sold by the yard with a muslin backing. It is also sold in loose bulk form for stuffing cushions completely and in bed-size sheets for padding quilts.

Super-soft foam is best for the main softening of a cushion. Use the batting—at most two or three wraps—to round edges and give a cushion height. Batting settles with use; if you overwrap cushions, they may "deflate" in time.

To give cushion edges and corners a very round effect, trim the foam at an angle along the edges before you wrap. To soften all edges, wrap from front to back as well as from side to side.

Secure wrapped batting around foam by handstitching the loose end to the batting layer beneath it.

Choosing a fabric

When selecting an upholstery fabric, you may consider its durability and appearance first of all. But these are not the only factors to think about. Here are a few other considerations:

Texture. Coarse fabrics snag clothing and are uncomfortable to sit on if you're wearing thin clothing. Slippery fabrics slide you away from back support. Choose fabrics that can breathe; if they can't, you'll perspire.

Textured fabrics with a nap—must be sewn with all the nap going in one direction. Sometimes this means buying extra fabric.

Washability. Washable fabrics are generally more desirable than those that must be dry cleaned, especially for outdoor use. Even better for maintenance are fabrics with spot-resistant finishes, soil-release finishes, and permanent-press finishes.

You should preshrink washable fabrics. Do this the same way you'll wash and dry the finished cover.

Patterned fabrics. Before you buy a print or striped fabric, visualize it on the completed project. If you choose a striped fabric, decide the direction of the stripes and determine whether you'll need extra fabric for matching the stripes. For patterned fabrics, plan to direct the pattern one way and decide whether or not you're going to match it. Compensate for this when you figure yardage.

Making cushions

A cushion isn't hard to define—it's just stuffing held by a fabric bag. The way you sew the bag together will make a difference in the cushion's shape. A discussion of the main types of cushions and how to make them follows:

A word about preparation: choose your method before buying the fabric—it can make a difference in the amount needed.

Preshrink the fabric (if washable) and cut it out carefully.

In the construction, be sure to allow for an opening large enough to push the stuffing through. And decide how you'll close that opening. If you use a zipper, hook-and-pile tape, or upholstery tape with snaps, install the device (according to manufacturer's directions) in its seam or panel before sewing remaining seams. Be sure any zipper you buy is rustproof.

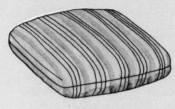

KNIFE-EDGE CUSHION

Making knife-edge cushions. The drawing above shows an example of a knife-edge cushion. This style is quite easy to make, but it has a less definite shape than the box cushion discussed at right.

Here's how:

1) Cut the two fabric halves and put them face to face. If you plan to install a zipper, sew it to the pieces first, following the directions on the package.

2) Stitch the fabric together along three sides, about ½" in from the edges.

3) Trim off excess seam allowance and turn the cover right side out. Stuff the cover.

4) If you didn't put in a zipper, close the opening with an overcast stitch.

MAKING A KNIFE-EDGE CUSHION

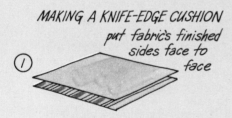

① put fabric's finished sides face to face

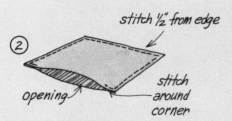

② stitch ½" from edge

opening   stitch around corner

③ turn right side out and stuff with foam

④ close opening with overcast stitch

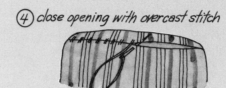

Making box cushions. These cushions have side panels that help maintain their rectangular shape. One is shown below. Box cushions are harder to make than knife-edge cushions.

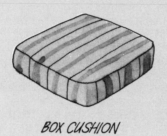

BOX CUSHION

Here's how:

1) Cut out the six pieces, allowing for a ½" seam allowance around all edges. Plan an extra ⅝" for each side of a zipper.

2) Install a zipper in one of the side panels, or plan for a similar closure.

3) Working on the wrong side of the fabric, sew the four side panels together end to end, allowing about ½" seams.

4) Sew the side panels to the top and bottom panels. Trim excess allowances.

5) Turn the cover right side out and fill it.

MAKING A BOX CUSHION

① six fabric pieces

② zipper or closure

③ sew side panels together

allow ½" seams

④ add top and bottom panels

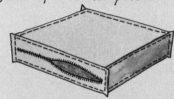

⑤ turn right side out and stuff with foam

Making drawstring covers. Bolsters and other round-form cushions can be covered with drawstring covers. These are very easy to make.

DRAWSTRING COVER

Here's how:

1) *For a one-opening cover,* as pictured on page 78, cut out a large circle of fabric. The circle's radius should equal the radius of your cushion, plus the cushion's depth, plus the distance the cover will tuck under the bottom, plus allowance for a casing (about 1"). Form a casing around the perimeter of the circle, easing fabric as needed to minimize puckering. Leave a ½" opening for the drawstring. (See page 76 for details on how to make a casing.)

For a cover open at both ends (as for a bolster), cut a strip of fabric the width of your cushion plus about 2" for two casings, and the length of your cushion's circumference plus about 1¼" (⅝" seam allowance at each end). Seam the two ends of the fabric together, forming a cylinder, and press the seam open. Form a casing at each end, leaving ½" opening for the drawstring.

2) Fasten a safety pin onto one end of the drawstring and fish it through the casing. Adjust the cord evenly once it's through. Tie a knot in each end.

3) Turn the cover right side out, slip it over the cylinder or stuffing, and pull the cord taut, gathering the fabric evenly. Tie the ends together and tuck them in the opening.

Covering irregular cushions. To cover cushions of unusual shapes, follow the instructions for box or knife-edge cushions. Make a paper pattern to fit the dimensions of the cushion form. To insure accuracy, test the pattern by making a sample cover from muslin or fabric scraps.

Sewing mitered corners (for knife-edge cushions). You can add a bit more distinction to knife-edge cushions by mitering the corners as shown in the drawing below. Here are two ways this can be done:

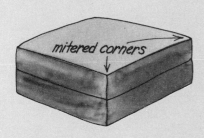

mitered corners

1) When the cover is inside out and stitched, fold it so the seams are centered on top of each other and pin the corners. Make the miter by sewing across the corners, perpendicular to the seam lines, 1½" to 3½" in from the corners. (The long side of the resulting triangle will determine the cushion's depth.) Trim the corner to eliminate bulk in the seam.

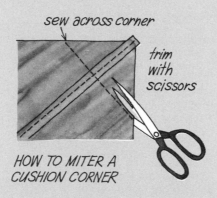

sew across corner

trim with scissors

HOW TO MITER A CUSHION CORNER

2) A folded miter can be made after the cushion cover is sewn and turned right side out. Simply fold the corner inside to make a neat pocket. Because sewing through several thicknesses of bulky fabrics or leather is difficult, this method works best for those materials.

Closing a cushion's opening. As previously mentioned, you have to decide early how you'll close the opening that you push the stuffing through. Install zippers and similar devices according to the directions on the package. If you're inexperienced, putting them in can be difficult; here are a couple of alternatives.

One simple solution is to allow extra fabric at the cushion's backside. From this fabric, make two overlapping fabric panels. Hem and overlap the two pieces 1½" to 3" before stuffing the cushion.

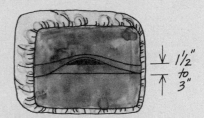

↓ 1½" to 3"

extra fabric at cushion's backside overlaps for an easy-to-make closure

The easiest way to close a cushion is to handstitch the last seam. Of course, to remove the cover, you must cut the seam open. The overcast stitch, shown in the drawing below, is strong, fast, and easy to master.

Another permanent closure is machine topstitching. After the cover is turned right side out and stuffed, fold in the raw edges of the unfinished seam and stitch both together, close to the edge, with a short machine stitch.

OVERCAST STITCH

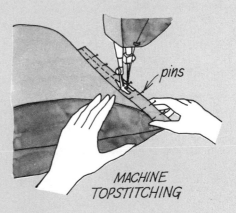

pins

MACHINE TOPSTITCHING

Index